Slovak
Touches

FAMILY RECIPES ✳ HISTORY ✳ FOLK ARTS

By Toni Brendel

✳

Penfield BOOKS

Front cover:
Laura Christine Satre, 20, granddaughter of the author and the late Richard Haas attends the University of Wisconsin–Eau Claire. Laura wears a *kroj* (folk dress) originally designed for her grandmother by relatives in the Spiš Region of Slovakia. Laura's great-great-grandmother was born there.

The beautiful headdress, called a *diadem* or *parta*, is adorned with three trailing embroidered ribbons. Smaller, bright colored bows are sewn onto braided fabric on either side of her headdress. In the center is a large ball of tiny metal springs and sequins. The circle frame is made from wood. A plain white blouse with full puffed sleeves is covered by a brocade vest over which a flowered, fringed scarf is worn. A long, full skirt with tiers of tiny tucks is hand-embroidered at the bottom and finished with pulled threads along the hemline. A white cotton apron with richly embroidered trim is tied in the back. Black boots complete her ensemble.

Back view of kroj *worn on front cover by Laura Christine Satre.*

Back cover and title page:
Stacey Michelle Erickson, 19, granddaughter of the author and the late Richard Haas attends the University of Wisconsin-Eau Claire. Stacey wears a *kroj* similar to that of her cousin, Laura. She wears the costume without the fringed shawl in order to show the lovely brocade vest. One-inch pleats create a lace-edged peplum at the bottom of the vest which flares slightly over the hips. These *kroje* are typical of the Spiš Region.

Front and back cover photography by Joan Liffring-Zug Bourret.

©2008 Toni Brendel
ISBN 9781932043495

Library of Congress 2008921101

Contents

Dr. Martin Mešša photograph

Slovak girls in kroje *from Spiš*

Dedication:

This book is dedicated in loving memory to six great women who impacted our lives beyond description: Velma Mráz-Brendel, Anna Mráz, Esther Schuster-Mráz, Emma Mráz-DeFabio, Margaret Mráz-Maleček, and Nettie Bejček-Mráz.

Acknowledgments

It is with deep appreciation and love I thank my cousins Paul Hudak, Michael and David DeFabio, Louise Scramuzzo-DeFabio, Dr. Ann Voda, Vicki Voda Weber, Robert Mráz, Lois Mráz Potratz, and my siblings and their spouses: Helen and Dick, Shirley and Carl, and Chuck and Sarah. Without their assistance and interest, the book would not have been written. With abiding love, I thank my children Tami, Valerie, Bill, Ryan, John, Scott, and Sandy, and grandchildren: Andrew, Laura, Grant, Stacey, Austin, and Eli for their love, humor, loyalty, and encouragement. Heartfelt thanks to friends Kathy Clemen, Bernice Polacek, Joan Tilma, Janet Beecham, Karen Baumgartner, Kathy Schilling, Karl, Marguerite, and Bill and Vernette Moravek for being there to cheer me on. Special thanks and love to Tim Irwin for his photographic assistance, advice, understanding, and kindness beyond expectation. Also, special thanks to the many others who contributed photographs.

Thanks to the wonderful people at ÚĽUV (Ústredie ľudovej umeleckej výroby—The Centre for Folk Art Production) in Bratislava, Slovakia, for opening the doors: Milan Beljak, ÚĽUV Director; Martina Straková, International Communications and Cultural Affairs Officer; Dr. Martin Mešša, for the ÚĽUV *kroje* photographs and Miro Pokorný, Jr., Day of Masters photography. Thank you to friends Darinka and Clayton Kohl, curators of the Wisconsin Slovak Museum in Cudahy, Wisconsin, and John Hosmanek, editor of the *Wisconsin Slovak* magazine, for making historical data available and being helpful in every way possible. Thanks to William Ivins, University of Pittsburgh, for his photo contributions, and to Joe Senko for his valuable assistance.

Thank you to CEO Gail Naughton and staff of the National Czech & Slovak Museum & Library in Cedar Rapids, Iowa, for informational and folk art contributions. Thanks to the directors, members, and photographers of the many wonderful Slovak dance groups. You are excellent ambassadors!

Artist, Editors, and Graphic Designers

Sarah Krueger created the line art illustrations in this book. A graduate of Lawrence College, Appleton, Wisconsin, she is enjoying retirement after teaching art for thirty-four years. She is a sister-in-law of Toni Brendel. Cover design is by Molly Cook of M.A. Cook Design. Editors included Joan Liffring-Zug Bourret, Dwayne Bourret, Melinda Bradnan, Miriam Canter, Dorothy Crum, David Heusinkveld, Deb Schense, Jacque Gharib, Connie Schnoebelen, John Johnson, David Trawick, David Wright, and Ivana Takáčová.

Preface

Although my Slovak maternal grandmother, Anna Broskova (Mráz), died before my birth, she heavily influenced the lives of my sisters, brother, and cousins. This influence filtered down through the Brosko-Mráz family line to her children, our parents. The early demise of my grandmother greatly affected her family. My mother spoke of her endearingly, indeed, to the end of her own life. As I grew older, I noted it was the same with my *Teta* Anna, and when the Mráz siblings came together en masse, the pattern was retraced. Perhaps it was the family's way of keeping her alive in their hearts, and took the edge off her being taken from their midst in such an untimely fashion.

Grandmother Anna was continually credited with being a devout Christian woman, a good manager with a good work ethic, a wonderful cook, and an attentive mother who weaned her children on age-old Slovak sayings and maxims. Reportedly blessed with a good disposition and sense of humor, many humorous tales trickled down through the family tree, nourishing our own branches and precipitating colorful leaves of humor in each of us.

In retrospect, although physically absent, we grew up knowing this grandmother. As my mother reminisced and my siblings and I assumed certain household chores, we came to know her through the ever-present "my mother said," and "my mother did it this way." This was true in baking, cooking, spring and fall house-cleanings, even to the humble chore of bed-making.

My mother's own indomitable spirit was credited directly to my grandmother. The resilience with which she met hardship, personal heartache, and tragedy was one of the many gifts she seemingly inherited and passed on. Her oft-used phrase, "My mother said you can get used to anything but hanging!" brought a smile to our lips and a nudge toward the reality that we could deal with unexpected or unwelcome change in our lives. With those words came comfort, and we "pulled ourselves up by the bootstraps," and went on. How could I not want to preserve the integrity of those grass roots qualities and pass them on?

The Phillips Czechoslovakian Community Festival founded in 1984 made me even more keenly aware of my heritage. The late Dr. August Jurischica, President of the Wisconsin Slovak Historical Society, urged the founders to preserve the history of Slovak and Czech immigrant families who settled in Price County at the turn of the century and beyond. I was part of that endeavor, and since my Slovak family settled in Price County during that time, I began to ask questions of my mother, aunts, and uncles to preserve the family history. It became increasingly apparent that the stories were worth the telling. So here, in *Slovak American Touches*, they are told.

—Toni Brendel

Slovakia, Beautiful Land

One of the smaller European countries, the Slovak Republic covers almost nineteen thousand square miles with a population of over five million. Eighty-five percent of the population is made up of ethnic Slovaks. Approximately one-tenth are ethnic Hungarians, with Romanies (Gypsies), the second largest minority group. Smaller minority groups include Ruthenians, Germans, Ukrainians, Poles, Jews, Czechs, Belarusians, and Italians.

Bratislava, the capital city, is located in the far southwestern corner of the country with over 450,000 residents. Nitra is the oldest city in Slovakia.

Widely mountainous, Slovakia offers rivers, thermal springs, lakes, and forests with a lush variety of flora and fauna. The Danube River provides outlets to the North and Black Seas. Other significant rivers include the Orava, Hornád, Nitra, Hron, Morava, and Váh.

Tourism bolsters the economy. Visitors from around the world come to fish, climb mountains, hike, bike, and participate in summer water sports. Cool, quiet respites in dense, thick forests provide welcome relief to city dwellers. Many native families spend weekends or holidays at cottages near lakes. Summer vacations are spent in the quiet environment of the country forests, where wild fruits, berries, and mushrooms grow abundantly. Mountain lakes and streams provide excellent sport for anglers. Thermal springs in twenty-three locations attract international visitors in search of wellness therapies and cures. Winter sports lure visitors during the long, cold, winter months. Tourist information centers have sprung up all over the country to assist those who wish to explore the many sightseeing opportunities in this beautiful country.

With thoughtful foresight, the Slovaks protected their natural resources. National parks and preserved areas are based in the High Tatra (Vysoké Tatry), Low Tatra (Nízke Tatry), the Little Fatra (Malá Fatra), Giant Fatra (Veľká Fatra), the Muráň Plain (Muránska Planina), Poloniny, the Upper Orava (Horná Orava), Štiavnica Hills, the Slovak Paradise, and the Slovak Karst. The High Tatra boasts the highest crest of the West Carpathian Mountain range, and is the location of the country's largest national park—its mountains creating the border between Poland and Slovakia. The highest point is Gerlach Peak at 2,655 meters above sea level. Seventeen other mountaintops in the area are only slightly lower than this height. A magnificent sight, the High Tatra is noted for its many valleys, with almost a hundred lakes created by ancient glacial activity. The edelweiss flower of "Sound of Music" fame flourishes in the High Tatra and is now a protected species. It is one of over a thousand types of plant life thriving in this mountainous terrain. In these elevated forests, it is common to see wildcats, marmot, deer, lynx, otters, chamois, and bears as well as a wonderful variety of birds.

In the Slovak Paradise (Slovenské Rudohorie) area, varied fauna are supported by a myriad variety of wild plant life. The beauty of the Malá Fatra region is considered one of Slovakia's better kept secrets. This mountain range is situated on the north side of the Váh River. Over thirteen hundred types of butterflies populate this heavenly region. The brown bear, peculiar to the area, is frequently sighted. This is also the location of the oldest-known ice cave in Europe. During forty years of Communist rule, tourism was not promoted, and the Slovak Paradise remained unspoiled. It now has become a popular site for those seeking panoramic views of massive mountains and their peaks, waterfalls, rivers, caves, and scenic valleys. Hiking and skiing are the most popular pastimes.

Tillage farming occupies almost half of Slovak land. Most of the remaining acreage is used for grazing animals. Potatoes, wheat, corn, sugar beets, sunflowers, hops, and tobacco are the most widely-grown crops. Fields of sunflower seeds are harvested and processed for oil and other products.

Beer production is important, and large Heineken breweries are located in Hurbanovo, Rimavská Sobota, and Nitra. These breweries produce almost half of the country's beer, with smaller, lesser-known breweries supplying the rest.

Commercial industry is also an important part of the Slovak economy. Mining, which developed along with wood, paper, glass, and textile manufacturing during the last half of the nineteenth century, is probably the most important. The country is rich in precious metals and minerals, with large deposits of copper, iron ore, lead, zinc, antimony, mercury, limestone, dolomite, and brown coal. The Academy of Mining, the first university of its kind in Europe, was established in Banská Štiavnica during the eighteenth century.

The Slovak legacy is a culture rich with tradition. Its music, dance, literature, poetry, visual arts, and craftsmanship complement the color and drama of the Slovak personality. Politically and culturally repressed for centuries, Slovaks somehow quietly managed to preserve and cherish their ancestral cultural identity. It was feared, by this writer at least, that modern technology would obliterate some of the astounding Slovak craftsmanship.

Following the historic, non-violent Czechoslovakian Velvet Revolution against the Soviet Union in 1989 and the peaceful Velvet Divorce of the Czech and Slovak peoples in 1993, entrepreneurs from around the world flooded into Slovakia to seek opportunities in industry and business. This rapid development was greatly aided by the initiation of democracy and the free enterprise system. The Slovaks embraced a new sense of pride in cooperation and ownership. Growth has been painful, the journey hard and slow, but the struggle has resulted in a new Slovakia rising from the ashes like the proverbial phoenix.

Historic Slovak Timeline

4000–50 BC
Permanent settlements sprang up in this area of Europe. Celtic tribes came and the Cotini tribe, part of the Púchov culture, settled in the north central part of Slovakia. The Celtic settlers are believed to be the first to mint coins here, thought to be silver in (present-day) Bratislava.

AD 500–863
Driving Celtic tribes out, Germanic Quadi tribes settled in Slovakia north of the Danube River. Slavic tribes arrived from east of the Carpathian Mountains. Frankish merchant Samo was chosen as king. They, in turn, were driven out by the forces of Attila the Hun. The first church was established in Nitra, Slovakia. Byzantine missionaries Cyril and Methodius, from Slavic speaking Macedonia in Northern Greece, wrote a new alphabet and enabled Slavs to worship God in their own tongue. This was "Old Slavic," recognized as one of four world liturgical languages which included Hebrew, Latin, and Greek.

870–1000
Great Moravia began to flourish. Slovakia (then East Moravia) was occupied by Hungarian tribes who ruled this part of Slovakia for over 1000 years. Great Moravia fell. Bavarians lost the battle of Bratislava. Magyars ran rampant and attacked various parts of Europe. The Magyars, nomadic horsemen who terrorized Europe for over 50 years, were defeated and settled along the Danube and the Theiss in the plains. A multi-ethnic Hungarian Kingdom, including Slovakia, was founded by King Stephen of the Arpad Dynasty. King Stephen was later canonized as St. Stephen.

1241–1543
Tatars invaded Hungary. Its rulers invited Germans to Slovakia and Transylvania. Many fortifications and castles were built to ward off attacks. Mining communities and cities were founded and old cities grew. Matúš Čák from Trenčín ruled most Slovak territory. Hussite era affected Slovaks when Taborite armies penetrated Slovakia after Hus's death. Hussite doctrines and Czech Bible disseminated among Slovaks. Universal education in place. Most everyone could read and write. The lands of Hungary were divided for 150 years with the central part in the hands of the Turks. The Habsburgs owned a crescent-shaped strip of land which included Slovakia, the most western part of Hungary and western part of Croatia. Bratislava became the administrative capital of the Habsburg-ruled portion of the Hungarian kingdom. Magyar-Slovak ethnic frontier shifted to the north. Migration of Magyar nobles helped weaken German patricians.

1608–1720

Hungarian chief in Bratislava challenged German supremacy and gave Germans, Hungarians, and Slovaks equal say in municipal power. Lutheran Reformation spread throughout Habsburg-ruled Hungaria and Transylvania, which prompted promotion of Catholicism by the Habsburgs. The Thirty Years' War. Central Europe was devastated.

Slovak national movement founded with aim of fostering sense of national identity. Codification of a Slovak literary language by Anton Bernolák.

1805–1918

Napoleon and his French army defeated Austrian, Prussian, and Russian armies in battle of Austerlitz in Moravia. Pillaging and destruction of Slovak lands followed. Formation of a standard Slovak language in writing. First dictionary of Slovak language by Ľudovít Štúr and fellow scholars. Slovak National Council was formed: termed *Slovak Awakening*. Members struggled for autonomous status within the Hungarian Empire.

The Austro-Hungarian Empire (1867–1918) was made up of two separate states. Austria ruled over Bohemia, Moravia, Austrian Silesia, Slovenia, and Austrian Poland. Hungary ruled what was known as Royal Hungary (which included Slovakia,) Transylvania, Croatia, and part of the Dalmatian Coast.

Thousands of citizens of Slovak lineage were consequently listed as Hungarians when they entered the United States during that time. As a result, many famous people of Slovak heritage were listed as Hungarians. Many Jewish people sailed to America prior to the larger migration of Slovaks who came to work in industrial cities and mines.

The assassination of Ferdinand D'Este, successor to the Austro-Hungarian throne and his Czech wife, Sofia, ignited World War I. In 1914 twenty-five percent of Slovak nation was in the USA. Slovaks in America assisted in struggle against "Hungarization" of Slovaks in Central Europe. Common state of Czechs and Slovaks sought. 1915, Cleveland Agreement; 1916, Pittsburgh Agreement. Slovak leader Milan R. Štefánik and Czech Tomáš G. Masaryk championed cause to unify Czechs and Slovaks for economic/political reasons. In 1918, they merged into one Czechoslovakia with Tomáš G. Masaryk as first President.

1937–1939

Death of President Masaryk (1937). Munich Agreement was forced on Czechoslovakia by French and English allies. Sudetenland, large areas of Bohemia and Moravia were ceded to Nazi Germany (September 1938). Vienna arbitration forced on Czech-Slovaks, ceding large land areas to Hungary (November 1938). All remaining Czech lands were taken over by Nazi Germany and referred to as Protectorate of Bohemia and Moravia. Slovakia proclaimed a puppet state run by a Catholic priest, Jozef Tiso. Jews were deported. Some Slovaks supported the state. Underground resistance movement gained strength.

1944–1948

The Slovak National Uprising in the city of Banská Bystrica against Nazi regime headquartered in Bratislava (August 29, 1944). Czechoslovakia liberated by Russians from the east and Americans from the west. Again, Slovak fate determined by foreign powers. President Beneš declared Decrees of Nationalization.

Most people of German lineage expelled to Germany. The 1946 elections placed Communist Party in power with 40 percent of vote; mostly in Czech lands. Catholic center parties strongest in Slovakia. The Czechoslovak Communist Party seized power (February, 1948). Private property nationalized. Farmers forced to join collective farms. Last of Eastern Europe's fledgling democracies reduced to satellite state. Communist Party made efforts to decrease influence of the Church.

1967–1989

Prague Spring Reform Movement. Alexander Dubček leads "communism with a human face." New freedoms gained fleetingly. Dubček expelled from Communist Party. Tight control took hold. Warsaw Pact armies invaded country (August 21, 1968). Head man Gustáv Husák, allowed no more reforms. Between 700,000–800,000 people fled the country.

Charter 77 published to demand fundamental human rights. Václav Havel, playwright, included among dissidents. Mass protests produce Velvet Revolution. Communist leader G. Husák resigned. Václav Havel appointed President of new Czech and Slovak Federated Republic. Democracy instituted.

1990–2007

Mass privatization of business and economic reforms swept Slovakia. First free and democratic elections held (June, 1990). Václav Havel elected President and Marián Čalfa, a Slovak, elected Vice President. New non-Communist Slovak government led by Vladimír Mečiar, a member of PAV (Public Against Violence), and in 1991, by Ján Čarnogurský, a leader of Christian Democratic Movement.

Vladimír Mečiar became Prime Minister of Slovakia. Czech and Slovak Federal Republic; dialogue began in Prague with Mečiar and Václav Klaus as figureheads. Velvet Divorce. The Czech and Slovak Federated Republics separated into two Republics to be known as Czech Republic and Slovak Republic (January 1, 1993). Michal Kováč elected Slovak President. Mečiar resigned as Prime Minister after a no confidence vote. Caretaker government led by Jozef Moravčík. Mečiar's newly formed party won at polls, and he was once again Prime Minister. Corruption and hostility toward minority groups isolated Slovakia from rest of world. Hungary and Slovakia signed treaty of cooperation.

Constitutional crisis arose. Vladimír Mečiar defeated at polls. New Prime Minister, Mikuláš Dzurinda. Election for President of Slovak Republic is held, and Rudolf Schuster was elected by the people. Slovakia invited to join OECD*.

Major redrafting of country's constitution; a key to gaining membership in EU and NATO. Regional parliaments created to gain entry to EU by constitutional amendment. Mikuláš Dzurinda became second term premier. Government formed center-right coalition. EU summit formally invites Slovakia to join in 2004. Slovaks went to referendum vote to favor EU membership. Slovakia admitted to NATO. Ivan Gašparovič elected President. Slovakia joined the EU. Slovakia plans to use European currency. Parliament ratified EU constitution. Robert Fico, left wing opposition leader, became prime minister. Announcement of Slovakian troop withdrawal from Iraq by February, 2007.

*Organization for Economic Co-operation and Development helping governments in a global economy.

Among The Famous Slovaks

Early Rulers and Kings

Prince Pribina (–861). Ruled the Principality of Nitra, which is present day Slovakia. Built the first Christian Church consecrated in 828. Died in battle against the Great Moravian Prince Rastislav in 861.

Prince Mojmír I (795–846). Defeated Prince Pribina. Became ruler of the Great Moravian Empire in 833. Succeeded by his nephew, Rastislav, in 846.

Matúš Čák III (1252–1321). Ruler of the Váh and Tatras Region. One of the greatest Slovak leaders. Died in Rozhanovce, battling the forces of King Charles I of Hungary.

Folklore Hero

Juraj Jánošík (1688–1713). Known as the Slovak Robin Hood, Jánošík touches the hearts of all Slovaks. Born in Terchová, many tales tell of his brief life, the boldness of his character. Allegedly, he was in the Hungarian Imperial Army, defected, was captured, and severely beaten. He reportedly hid in the mountains, becoming chief to a band of outlaws. Credited with eleven robberies, he never committed murder. He robbed from the rich and gave to the poor, endearing him to the Slovak peasants. Noted for bravery, at the young age of 25, he died a cruel death rather than betray his friends. A statue stands to his memory in Terchová.

Politicians and More

Ľudovít Štúr (1815–1856). Organizer of the National Revolution of 1848. Developed the modern Slovak language, and is known as poet, journalist, publisher, teacher, philosopher, linguist.

Milan Rastislav Štefánik (1880–1919). Played large part in Slovakian independence from Hungary and the formation of Czechoslovakia. Also a scientist, astronomer, and general in French Army.

Andrej Hlinka (1864–1938). Father of the Slovak nation. Catholic priest; co-founded the Slovak People's Party in 1905. Sought rights for Slovakian people.

Alexander Dubček (1921–1992). Communist Party leader, promoted "socialism with a human face" during the political reform movement, the "Prague Spring" in 1968, which brutally ended when the Soviet Union invaded Czechoslovakia. Expelled from the party, he was a political "non-person" for nearly two decades, then became Chairman of the Federal Assembly during the Velvet Revolution.

Felix Frankfurter (1882–1965). Considered one of the most important American lawyers and judges; appointed to the United States Supreme Court. Close advisor to Presidents Woodrow Wilson and Franklin D. Roosevelt. His family came from Bratislava.

Inventors

Jozef Karol Hell (1713–1789). Invented water pump machine in 1749, and was instrumental in developing the Banská Štiavnica silver mining operations.

Carleton Daniel Gajdušek (1923–). Co-recipient of Nobel Prize in medicine. Discovery of viruses with prolonged incubation period.

Jozef Maximilián Petzval (1807–1891). Invented camera zoom lens, and is considered a founder of modern photography.

Ján Bahyl (1865–1916). Inventor of steam tank and motor-driven helicopter. Acquired patents for air balloons combined with air turbine; petrol engine car (with Marschall).

Rev. Jozef Murgaš (1864–1929). Devised system which improved Morse Code, "Wireless Telegraph Apparatus." In 1904, provided foundation for invention of the radio. In 1905, he achieved radio transmission. Gave Marconi all rights.

Edward Teller (1908–2003). Born in Budapest, Teller helped develop the first atomic bomb and first hydrogen bomb. His father came from Nové Zámky, Slovakia.

Eugene Andrew Čerňan (1934–). An aeronautical engineer, Čerňan piloted the *Gemini* space craft in 1966 and the moon module *Apollo* in 1969. He led the *Apollo 17* team in 1972, and was the eleventh earth man to step on the moon.

The Arts

Master Pavol of Levoča (1470–). Most significant Gothic sculptor. Creator of Gothic High Altar in St. James Church in Slovakia, which is the highest wooden altar in the world.

Pavol Országh Hviezdoslav (1849–1921). Poet, playwright, and translator.

Béla Bartók (1881–1945). Brilliant Hungarian pianist and composer.

Max Reinhardt (1873–1943). Famous theater director who founded the Salzburg Festival in Austria. Baden native of Slovak ancestry.

J. Pola Negri (1897–1987). Famous star of motion pictures. Was a reigning queen of the Hollywood silent screen in German-made films.

Peter Lorre (1904–1964). Famous Hollywood actor from Ružomberok, Slovakia. Attained fame playing "bad guy" roles. Appeared in *Casablanca*.

Andy Warhol (1928–1987). Famous pop artist. First to use photographic silk-screen technique. He also used multiple images of the same person. While his people came from Slovakia, they were of Rusyn origin, an ethnic minority.

Paul Newman (1925–). Famous American movie actor and director. Creator of *Newman's Own* food products, which donates all proceeds to charity. Born of Slovak mother from Humenné.

Edita Grúberová (1946–). "Queen of Coloratura," internationally-known Slovak soprano.

Jozef Ivaška (1949–). International singing star, composer, "Man of a Thousand Songs." Born in Ružomberok, Slovakia. Graduate of Bratislava Conservatory of Music, the Faculty of Music, Institute of Music Arts in Bratislava, and University of Music and Performing Arts, Vienna. Chosen 2007 Cultural Ambassador of Slovakia by Slovaks living abroad.

Business

Morris Rich (1847–1928). Established large department store in Georgia which was first of its kind in America. Gained wide popularity with excellent treatment of employees and liberal credit policy. Rich was a native of Košice.

Daniel Hertz (1879–1961). Born in Vrútky, Slovakia, Hertz founded the Yellow Cab Company in Chicago, Illinois, and in 1954, he established the Hertz Corporation, which has car rental agencies worldwide.

Social Sciences

Bruno Bettelheim (1903–1990). Of Slovak ancestry, he became famous for his work with mentally challenged children and the emotionally disturbed.

Sports

Andrew Pafko (1921–). He played centerfield for three major league baseball teams during a 17-year career: Chicago Cubs (1943–'51), Brooklyn Dodgers (1951–'52), and Milwaukee Braves (1953–'59). He was named to five all-star teams and was recognized for both his infield and outfield prowess. Andrew, a devout Slovak Lutheran, is a member of Zion Evangelical Lutheran Church in Norridge, Illinois. The following is a firsthand account of meeting Andy Pafko by Toni Brendel.

Meeting Andy Pafko

A visit to cousins Paul and Bess Hudak, on April 13, 1997, provided a special bonus. Son Ryan and I attended a church service at the Hudak's home church in Norridge, Illinois. Since his father was to be honored for 50 years of church service, Pastor David Hudak absented himself from his own pulpit to attend the special occasion. Before the service began, I sat quietly perusing the bulletin and noted an Andrew Pafko was to read scripture that day.

Irreverent as it was, I couldn't resist leaning over Cousin David to get Paul's attention. "Is that the Andy Pafko who played baseball for the Milwaukee Braves?" I whispered. Paul likewise leaned over David and said, "No, the Chicago Cubs!" I shook my head and said, "No, the Braves!" David became involved and whispered, "Who's Andy Pafko?" I said, "He played for the Braves when they won the pennant in Milwaukee in 1957!" Paul, *sotto voce*, said, "No, he played with the Cubs when they played in the World Series!"

The church service began, and I was beside myself. I very clearly remembered the series in Milwaukee in 1957, as I lived there at the time. I knew who played on the team! My father was a great baseball player and fan. He managed the home town baseball team after he no longer played the game.

Our family was spoon-fed baseball, and he and mother came to Milwaukee to attend that series! Andrew Pafko read the scriptures, and I recognized him for who he was.

Later, after the service, Paul received his award. At a reception afterwards, Ryan and I met and visited with the famous Andy Pafko! We met his lovely wife, and each of us was given a baseball card autographed on the spot. He even provided a third card for my brother Chuck! Cousin Paul later told me he and Andy had been friends for many years. He had indeed played for the Chicago Cubs, the Brooklyn Dodgers, AND the Milwaukee Braves!

Slovak American Ties

According to the 2000 U.S. Census, 797,764 people of Slovak descent were living in the United States. The state of Pennsylvania represented the largest population with 243,009, with most concentrated in the western part of the state. Because of this, the Slovak Embassy opened an Honorary Consulate in Pittsburgh, in 1997. Joseph T. Senko was named Honorary Consul. He formed a non-profit organization, Western Pennsylvania Slovak Cultural Association. Its mission is to bring authentic Slovak cultural programs to Western Pennsylvania for the public to enjoy. These programs and artists must come directly from Slovakia as representatives of the rich cultural talent that exists in that nation. The aim is to keep the programming highly diversified and appealing to a wide audience.

Approximately 100,000 Slovak Americans live in the Cleveland area. This city was cited as having the largest concentration of Slovaks in the early 1900s. During the 1970s the Slovaks were the largest immigrant group in that area with an estimated population of 48,000.

Many organizations throughout America were created to preserve the culture and traditions of Slovakia. Some were identified by names given during the time when the Czech Republic and Slovakia were one country, Czechoslovakia. While some have been renamed since the two nations became sovereign states in 1993, others were originally founded expressly for Slovaks in America. These groups met specific community needs. For many, these cultural associations, fraternal unions, and religious societies continue to keep the Slovak heritage alive today.

The National Czech & Slovak Museum & Library in Cedar Rapids, Iowa, has undertaken the task of maintaining a current listing of Slovak organizations in America. The most current information is found at the Museum & Library's website: www.ncsml.org

There are approximately one hundred organizations in the United States that recognize, promote, and foster ties with Slovak tradition. In perusing the roster of clubs and their mission statements, one realizes attempts are made through various means to partner in the growth and economy of the relatively new nation of Slovakia. Members of these organizations reach out with sponsorships, scholarships, other forms of assistance, and extend open arms to those who emigrate and those who remain in the land of their ancestors.

To promote and preserve the Slovak heritage in the United States, the Slovak American Cultural Center was founded in New York City in 1967 as a non-profit organization. By providing lectures, seminars, concerts, and many cultural events, it gave the New York, New Jersey, and Connecticut Slovaks the opportunity to socialize and preserve their rich cultural heritage.

In the late 1980s, the Center started a "Heart to Heart" program to sponsor advanced medical education for pediatric cardiology. Through the program, several Slovak cardiologists were trained in the U.S.A. and the U.K. This eventually enabled specialized medical care for the entire Slovak Republic and neighboring countries.

Since 1993, cultural groups concentrating on educational pursuits and reciprocal fine arts exchanges with Slovakia have sprung up around the nation; some even before. These groups representing the Slovak population are common in the eastern states of Maine, Maryland, Massachusetts, New Jersey, New York, Pennsylvania, Washington D.C., and Virginia. There is also a distinctive presence in Arizona, California, Florida, Illinois, Indiana, Iowa, Kansas, Nebraska, Michigan, Minnesota, Missouri, Ohio, Oklahoma, South Dakota, Texas, and Wisconsin.

Many of the clubs are purely social, extending a warm welcome to those of the same nationality who wish to bond with kindred spirits. These gatherings are a good source for sharing news, dining on ethnic foods, polka dancing, and keeping Slovak tradition alive.

Among dozens of fraternal benefit societies is the First Catholic Slovak Ladies Association, first established in 1892 in Cleveland, Ohio. Prominent in twenty-one states of the Union and with a membership of over ninety thousand across the country, this fraternal society remains true to its mission: offering youth scholarships, caring for the sick and needy, and exercising patriotism.

Major universities across the nation sponsor international studies groups with a Slovak faction represented among foreign students. The Slovak Studies program at the University of Pittsburgh is the most noted. The Cleveland Slovak School for Children offers Slovak language classes for children beginning at 4 years of age. Slovak Studies at John Carroll University, University Heights, Ohio, has a formal Slovak language program. In 1999, the university dedicated a Slovak Heritage Room in Gasselli Library with funding by the First Catholic Slovak Ladies Association and the First Catholic Slovak Union.

Genealogy societies are active in many states and assist in genealogical searches for members, tracing roots back to ancestral lands. A large membership from all over the United States, as well as several foreign countries, reap benefits from The Czechoslovak Genealogical Society International (CGSI) in Minnesota. Many have been reunited with family members in Slovakia through its services.

Dance groups preserve the folk dances and music of Slovakia and entertain large audiences throughout the United States.

A fine vehicle to keep youth interested in heritage is the Miss Czech-Slovak US Queen Pageant, held the first weekend of August in Wilber, Nebraska. Founded by John and Lois Fiala, of Lincoln, Nebraska, the pageant provides an educational experience for all who take part in it. With a recent representation from twenty-one states, this annual contest continues to grow.

16

Special Slovak American Publishers

Helene and Helen

The Bolchazys

Helene Baine Cincebeaux and her mother, Helen Baine, founded the Slovak Heritage & Folklore Society International in 1986, which reaches over 1,600 families around the world with the quarterly magazine, *Slovakia*. A periodical with great versatility, it appeals to those who seek information on Slovak history, culture, music, art, folk dress, customs, crafts, and genealogy.

Helene authored *Treasures of Slovakia 1969–1990,* which contains photographs of the Slovak land, its customs and people. *Slovak Pride* contains 27,000 ancestral surnames and the villages where they can be found; it has connected many people with long-lost family in Slovakia and in America. Helene embraces the culture of her ancestors in a warm and personal way.

Dr. Lou and Dr. Marie Bolchazy founded the Slovak American International Cultural Foundation, Inc., in Wauconda, Illinois. A non-profit educational and charitable entity, its mission is to showcase the literary, artistic, and scholarly contributions of Slovaks and Slovak Americans to the world; and to provide editorial, technical, marketing, and financial assistance to publishers in Slovakia.

Dr. Lou Bolchazy received the Slovak National Award from Slovak President Ivan Gašparovič for seeking out Slovak writers and artists and furnishing assistance in publishing their works. He is the president of Bolchazy-Carduzzi Publishers, Inc. Both Bolchazys received the Illinois Classical Conference Lifetime Achievement Award for scholarship, teaching, and promotion of literary classics throughout the world.

The Chancery Building of the Embassy of the Slovak Republic, opened in 2001 in Washington D.C., was designed by Bogar Fischer Králik Lizon Urban of Slovakia.

Three Generations
In Slovakia, Milan Šuvada was visited by his daughter, Sonka Šuvadová Tostrud, right, and granddaughter, Sonia Riečanová, dance directors of Moja Vlasť Folklórny Súbor *(My Homeland Folk Group) Czech-Slovak Dancers of Milwaukee.*

ÚĽUV
Slovakia's National Cultural Institution

In my hunger to know more about my grandparents' origins, I looked for whatever I could find about Slovakia. Imagine my delight in discovering, on the Internet, the cultural organization, ÚĽUV, *Ústredie ľudovej umeleckej výroby* (The Centre for Folk Art Production). This organization, established and dedicated to the preservation and development of folk art in Slovakia, is supported by the Ministry of Culture of the Slovak Republic. Programs include art courses, exhibitions, sales of folk art, and the development and design of related products. ÚĽUV also maintains a large library and publishes titles of wide appeal. A chain of stores located throughout Slovakia sells folk art and crafts, which are also taught and produced at central locations.

In Bratislava, the Regional Centre of Crafts, located at 64 Obchodná Street, contains a gallery with permanent exhibitions dedicated to contemporary folk art, craft-related design, and creative folk art. The same address houses the Regional Centre of Crafts, which is the educational extension of the ÚĽUV group, with instruction for regional artists and artisans. The Design Studio, also in Bratislava at 13 Dobrovičova Street, exhibits small-scale works by Slovak artists and designers. The main focus (traditional techniques of craftsmanship and the preservation of heritage crafts) is supplemented with lively displays of contemporary work by younger contributors. In May 2005, the city of Banská Bystrica initiated its ÚĽUV operation and began to offer exhibitions of traditional folk art, supplemented with creative workshops, lectures, and guided tours. As if an answer to my prayer, the craftsmanship, art, and culture of the Slovak people are today being preserved, honored, promoted, and shared.

In the interest of preserving the traditional folk art of the Slovak people, the Centre of Folk Art Production was established in Bratislava in 1945. This came about through Presidential Order. In 1954, the entity was restructured under the supervision of the Ministry of Culture. Its activities, thereafter, focused on the cultural and social function of folk art production. Since that time, ÚĽUV exhibitions have provided cultural activity in 28 countries of the world. The Centre has built several show rooms and shops, and a cafeteria for visitors has been included on premises. Six decades ago, the vision of the founders was to save the Slovak culture and traditions created hundreds of years ago by their ancestors.

After six decades, the vision is enhanced and perpetuated by numerous craftsmen, artists, and experts in various branches of the field of art production. Seasoned experts join hands with new talent to save and revitalize techniques that were bordering on extinction. Workshop classes are now held so that masters may pass on knowledge only created through hands-on experience. The list of educational opportunities offered to learn traditional crafts is long and varied.

Research, documentation, manufacturing, and marketing have become important facets of the ÚĽUV's business. Their documentation material contains close to 16,000 artifacts, including three-dimensional objects constructed of traditional materials. These serve as a study base for modern-day designers. Approximately 1,300 craftspeople are registered in ÚĽUV and produce products made from corn, roots, straw, wicker, horn, clay, leather, metal, and wood. Many of these craftsmen work out of their homes and create a giant cottage industry while preserving the traditions of the Slovak people. Embroidery work, tatting, crocheting, other lace making, honey cakes, glass paintings, and decorated Easter eggs are added to the array of handiwork provided by these workers. The use of wool, linen, cotton fabrics, and blue-and-white print are intertwined in the make-up of the Slovak tradition and find their way to the market place by way of bolts of fabric and ready-made garments.

The Information and Education Center based at the main Bratislava location in the Crafts Courtyard enables visitors to learn of the many activities, shows, publications, and materials offered by the organization. In 1992, ÚĽUV became a member of the International Organization of Folk Art (IOFA) of UNESCO and, in 1993, with assistance from IOFA members, an international meeting "Models of Folk Art and Craft Preservation" took place in Dolná Krupá, Slovakia. In 1994, ÚĽUV became a member of the European Federation of Folk Arts and Crafts and published the Folk Art and Craft News, available in English and German.

In 1995, ÚĽUV became a member of the International Commission of Folk Art and Crafts. Milan Beljak, the Director of ÚĽUV, was elected the vice-president of the European Federation of Folk Arts and Crafts. One hopes that the original vision and ideals will be upheld and continue to flourish.

Preservation of Slovakian folk art at ÚĽUV also includes the reproduction of authentic national folk dress known as *kroj(e)*. Since the 1950s, a large quantity of *kroje* have been produced annually for folk groups, choirs, and dancers. While care is taken to authenticate details of the colorful creations, some modifications are made to incorporate garment wearability and longer life. With each region having a different style *kroj*, the archives at the Centre hosts an abundant inventory of variant national folk dress. Approximately ninety different designs are known.

Wood Etching

This type of etching was traditionally carved into wood, but in some areas of West and Central Slovakia etching was even used on Easter eggs. In the eastern part of Slovakia, horn was decorated by this means. Traditionally, it is considered a newer decorative technique. Zvolen and Detva are two towns that are noted for this artistic offering. Musical instruments, laundry tools, distaffs, mangleboards, shepherds' sticks, bowls, spoons, and ladles are the most popular examples of this type of decorative work. Shepherds' long pipes and whistles are considered rarities.

Woodcarving

Used in folk architecture, carved products have been part of the ÚĽUV collections since its inception. Traditional folk patterns found their way into the decoration of various pieces of furniture, tools, dishes, butter, and honey cake molds, pillars, and posts. Figures carved of wood were often used to decorate wooden beehives that dot the Slovakian landscape. The richest of all woodcarvings are found in churches and old castles around the countryside. These carving techniques are now being preserved by the local artisans.

Barrel Making

The occupations of wine production, cheese making, brewing, mining, and tanning made the use of barrels widespread in Slovakia. Additionally, most village households contained numerous casks and barrels used for the storage of foods and other household goods. Today, products traditionally made by coopers appear demonstrated in smaller dimensions, such as casks, wash-tubs, buckets, and churns. Some are produced in miniature to give the viewer an idea of traditional wares.

Wood Splitting

The art of splitting wood in fine slices and the technique used to weave baskets and hanging ornaments is preserved today. Split pieces of wood do not break easily; durability is ensured for solidity and prolonged use. Wood shingles were made by wood splitting, and, in earlier years, the wheelwright's trade was dependent on it. In the 1960s, lampshades with carved designs were introduced and became a more modern form of wood splitting offered by modern artists. In the town of Kyjatice, the technique is used in making furniture and toys. This art form is widely used in folk settings and is being taught at ÚĽUV centers.

Chiselling

For more than three decades, chiselled-wood products have been produced by artists at ÚĽUV. Axe work or chiselling was the main occupation of a group of Romanians who came to Eastern Slovakia during the second half of the nineteenth century. Troughs, bowls, spoons, and wooden kitchen utensils, including dippers, spoons, and scrapers are the most popular made at the present time.

Woodturning

Tools used for weaving, various parts of furniture, whistles, toys, kitchen bowls, and plates were all made by woodturning. The art of woodturning was prevalent in all of Slovakia but in some villages more than others, as some made it a source of income. At the end of the 1960s, younger woodturners devised new products. Salt cellars, candles sticks, bowls, plates, and small storage boxes appeared on the market. These items were often combined with chased metal inlay, patterns burned with the use of hot wire or nitric acid, or stained with mordants. Combined with glass paintings or metallic parts, beautiful smooth wooden utilitarian, as well as decorative items, were created.

Metal Decoration

Using folk jewelry in traditional form as their guide, artists at the Centre fashioned new creative designs in metal jewelry. A permanent part of the ÚĽUV experience, coining, engraving, and cutting (traditionally used in making folk jewelry) are recognized as representative of the techniques used by earlier craftsmen. Along with this comes decorating the pieces to embellish and adorn, making each one unique. Old brooches, buckles, combs, rings, and clasps are modified to appeal to today's market, yet capture the charm of the original technique.

Cast Metals

The making of bells and ornamentations was grounded in northern Slovakia, but the techniques were known throughout Europe. Clasps, buttons, buckles, rings, and hair ornamentation were commonly cast. Small bells used to locate cattle, rattles, small jingle bells, large cathedral bells, and medium-sized dinner bells were produced in large quantities and lasted through the ages. The traditional uses and techniques of the production of cast metals are preserved at ÚĽUV. The artifacts exhibiting this art form are in the archives on site in Bratislava.

Chased Metal Inlay

Well known in the north and east regions of Slovakia, less prevalent in the western part, use of chased metal inlay was originally functional. Sheet-metal was used in the process, and the inlay connected cracked parts of wood or reinforced objects that got rigorous daily use. The technique is also used to enhance musical instruments such as whistles, bagpipes, and shepherds' long pipes, and to bolster and strengthen hatchet sticks, whips, hafts for knives, and distaffs. Along with the traditional products, a new line of non-traditional items has been introduced. In the 1950s, the decoration of caskets began. Designers are continually creating new objects in this medium and new designs for jewelry, ornaments, and cutlery are being created.

Cast Metals in Wood

A technique used initially as a utilitarian means, the casting of metal in wood was used to reinforce parts of wooden objects under stress. This means of using wood and metal was especially dominant in the northern part of Central and East Slovakia and north of West Slovakia. Traditionally, it was used to strengthen knife handles, bagpipes, distaffs, shepherds' sticks, and whips. Although it is still used to make the old products, today it is more widely used for decorative purposes. Ornate boxes, jewelry, knives, and containers are designed with the artistic value based on the contrast of the wood and metal colors.

Cornhusk creators, Day of Masters, Bratislava

Cornhusk Weaving and Cornhusk Dolls

In 1957, the Centre made contact with producers of traditional cornhusk weaving in the southern parts of Slovakia. A relatively new craft, it had its beginning in the second half of the nineteenth century. Mats, baskets, trivets, caskets, flasks, hats, sandals, and bags are included in the line. Today new techniques are being used by modern artists to introduce new color designs. Cornhusk dolls are typical Slovak products and characterize the Slovak way of life. Dolls have been created by modern-day artists in scenes depicting peasant and shepherd environments, in the absence of the traditional designs that have not yet been found.

Cane Products

Cane plants are found in abundance in the swampy areas of Southern Slovakia. The process by which canes were successfully used for mats and roofing material has become a lost art, but the Centre hopes to reestablish craft production discontinued in the 1970s.

Basket Making

Wicker was commonly used for basket weaving in Slovakia. Willow wicker could be used either peeled, unpeeled and green, or in a refined state. Baskets used for potatoes, laundry, poultry, and large corn drying baskets were frequently those made of the green wicker. When basket-making schools became fashionable, the more refined wicker was used to make better quality basketry. Refined (boiled) rods are used by basket weavers at the Centre, and new designs and patterns are being used along with old techniques for construction.

Weaving of Straw
Straw was commonly used for basket weaving. In Western Slovakia and in Central Slovakia's southern part, straw baskets were more detailed and refined. These baskets were more for bread dough use, but other baskets were also woven. In the middle of the twentieth century, ÚĽUV established a relationship with straw weavers in Western Slovakia. A unique technique of processing is used for straw ornaments and home decorations. Old techniques are used to offer new and original designs of baskets, straw ornaments, and home decorations at ÚĽUV Centres.

Splint-Basket Making
The woods in Central Slovakia are full of deciduous trees and prime for gathering material to make splint baskets. In the mid-1950s, producers of this type of basket began an association with designers from the Art Centre. Although work with splints was primarily a basketry type of art, spoon racks, sieves, cradles, portable beds, and other household items were made as well. Traditional baskets are still made, along with contemporary designs suggested by staff designers.

Root Weaving
Of all the natural basket weaving material, roots from pine, acacia, or fir trees are the hardiest. Using this type of material through the ages, the Záhorie region of West Slovakia, Northeast, and Northern Slovakia produced most of this type of basketry until the first half of the twentieth century. In the 1950s, producers from the Záhorie region and Northeast Slovakia began a partnership with the Centre and shared their expertise. Today, traditional baskets are still being made, but in smaller shapes and sizes than the original ones.

Embroidery
The Centre is striving to preserve the entire variety of techniques used in embroidery work in all sections of the country. Techniques and patterns vary greatly with each region. In the west, its hallmark is pre-painted embroidery; in the central part of the nation, more canvas embroidery is seen. Eastern region *kroj* finds less use of embroidery work. Domestic fabrics and *kroj* ornamentation using embroidery work affords significant evidence of location and origin of folk costumes. Traditional and new patterns are being used at the Centre.

Lace Making

The largest production of lace making took place in Kremnica, Banská Štiavnica, and Prešov. During the nineteenth century, each of those cities had lace-making workshops and schools. Bobbin lace and mining lace techniques were taught and the work of lace makers took on a professional look. Peasant lace was developed in the western regions. Lace making played an important role in the development of traditional textiles and is used on household linens and clothing, including folk costume trims. Traditional elements are preserved, and are taught at the Centre along with new varieties.

Miro Pokorný, Jr., Day of Masters photography

Lace Making, Day of Masters, Bratislava

Weaving

Through the ages, Northern Slovakia produced high-quality linen cloth and Eastern Slovakia was an important weaving region. For many centuries, manual production of woven fabrics was a domestic task that fell to every household. The woolen fabrics woven in all of Slovakia had a unified character and were most usually used as bedding. Rag rugs, window coverings, tablecloths, and pillows were needed to furnish homes and were created by the occupants themselves.

The traditional character of the woven fabrics was kept in most cases by

Day of Masters weaver

designers at the Centre, but a second direction is represented by items based on present-day needs. Applying the open-work technique used in Eastern Slovakia enabled designers to create textile collections for modern households. A technique used to make *"Guba"* cloth used woolen tufts twisted in during the weaving process. The original use for this type of fabric was to furnish coats for shepherds and coachmen, especially in the southeastern part of Slovakia.

When ÚĽUV craftsmen got involved with weaving products in the late 1950s, woolen rugs and upholstery fabric with rib weave were the only items made. Today, new designs of carpets and covers, small rugs, cushions, and women's coats have been introduced and made available at the Centre.

Blue-and-White Print

The eighteenth century marked the advent of traditional blue-and-white print prevalent in Northern and Central Slovakia. It became popular in the folk environment in the second half of the nineteenth century. At that time blue-and-white print workshops became sources of income for many villagers in those regions. Skirts, aprons, scarves, tablecloths, place mats, and other decorative materials were made from it. At the time it enjoyed popularity, almost every village had favorite patterns. Fabrics of blue with yellow, green, orange, light blue, and the traditional dark blue-and-white were commonly used. Only one representative makes this fabric today for the Centre, and the fabric is mostly used for clothing and domestic fabrics. New ideas have been introduced, and the blue-and-white print is being used in the production of toys, ornaments, and greeting cards.

Weft Twining

Sometimes called the cuff technique, weft twining was used mostly in the foothill regions and upland in Slovakia. Gloves, mules, and cuffs were the most common products, mostly used by forest workers and shepherds. Weft twining is produced at the Centre today for clothing, accessories for the home, and woolen rugs and cushions.

Weaving with a Rigid Heddle

This type of ancient weaving was still being produced in some small villages in the mid-twentieth century. Long narrow tapes were made with this technique and used for folk costume ties and decoration. Wider tapes used for shoulder straps, belts, bucket and basket handles, bookmarks, sheet webbing, and *kroj* decorations are still being produced today.

Knitting

In past years, knitting was something men did. During long hours of tending sheep, it was a common pastime. In the mountain regions, the knitted *"kopytcia"* was a type of footwear made of wool and put into leather shoes, or lined with leather or cloth. Gloves, cuffs, sweaters, and costumes created by modern artists match traditional designs.

Kraslice–Egg Decorating

Many techniques of egg decorating are preserved and taught at ÚĽUV. Included are wire netting, studding, batik, scratching, etching, gluing bits of straw, dyeing, and wax decoration.

Leather Products

The production of leather goods existed in all parts of Slovakia. Shoes, boots, belts, girdles, and bags were made of cowhide and were most widely constructed and worn for everyday use. Tobacco bags, girdles for fastening clothes, and cuffs and knife cases were not in demand and were made in smaller quantities. Interesting sewing techniques were used with shoemaker's thread and sometimes leather straps. The two groupings that are used today include traditional girdles, light footwear, folk costume belts, and shepherd's bags; those contemporary in style include handbags, belts, hold-alls, cases, and covers.

Horn Crafting

In 1956, an association with horn crafters was made by ÚĽUV artisans, and traditional decoration techniques were learned. Large and small cattle horns were used and artists painted scenes on the finished horn products. Some of the most interesting items came from the southern parts of Slovakia. Small cases, scythe sharpeners, utensils for filling sausage, and instruments used for pot painting were produced. Traditional wares and contemporary designs continue to be made at ÚĽUV.

Glass Painting

When the glassworks industry began to make glass panes in the eighteenth and nineteenth centuries, glass-painting was introduced. The first painters were from glassmaking families, and they painted to make extra income. Western Slovakian jug makers also painted this type of picture on glass. Glass painting was becoming a lost art in the 1950s, but artisans came forward and this art form is now being honored and preserved at ÚĽUV.

The Tinker's Trade

Specifically a Slovak craft, it originated in the eighteenth century. The trade was popularized in northwestern and northeastern Slovakia. Slovak tinkers exhibited their mastery in other European countries, in the U.S.A. and even Asia. It began as a way to mend broken pottery dishes, but then became an art unto itself. Household objects such as trivets, irons, baskets, bowls, and decorative items were later produced. The tinker's trade reached its pinnacle in the 1850s and began to decline after 1918. By 1945, it ceased to exist, but the tradition of tinker's production is maintained at the Bratislava Centre.

The Blacksmith's Trade

The village blacksmith was popular the world over and filled needs specific to rural areas, as well as cities. Since the advent of mass production and power driven tools, the craft is now extinct. No longer necessary to make tools, forge metal objects, repair carts and wagons, and fashion farm equipment, modern day blacksmiths make racks, fireplace tools, and decorative items at ÚĽUV.

Pottery

Pottery was an art form common to Slovakia. Serving and cooking dishes were most often produced. Pottery on display and in archives at ÚĽUV are copies of old ware modified or of new designs. Bardejov, Pozdišovce, Držkovce, and Sivetice are the original regions where traditional Slovak pottery was made.

Miro Pokorný, Jr., Day of Masters photography
Day of Masters potter

Majolica
Production of majolica was developed in Kostolná, Boleráz, Dobrá Voda, Dechtice, Sobotište, and Veľké Leváre. Workshops in these centers closed down in the nineteenth century. New artists became interested in pottery in the 1970s, and a younger generation continues to bring fresh ideas to new products.

Honey Cakes
Honey cake baking was once popular in the Bratislava area and in mining towns of Eastern and Central Slovakia. No longer produced from wooden molds, metal pastry cutters are now used and honey cakes are decorated with colorful drawings, at ÚĽUV.

Kroje Folk Attire
In Slovakia, typical folk dress was impacted by employment and climate. A wide spectrum of employment prevailed in the Spiš region. *Kroje* were made from natural basic raw materials including flax, fur, leather, and wool, which was provided by large herds of sheep. Styles were simple and unadorned. Folk costumes retained

their original character for centuries, but economic growth during the second half of the nineteenth century affected change. More expensive fabrics became available to the masses and replaced traditional flax, linen, and plainer cloth. Clothing worn for festive occasions became more stylish and ornate. Brocades, satins, and rich embroideries became popular and found their way into female attire.

In Závadka, Slovakia, elderly women often wear *kroje* for every day wear and a handful of them still practice the folk art custom of *kroj* making. Modern day women usually wear *kroje* only on festive holidays. The sleeves of the *kroj* blouse worn in the village of Závadka are puffed with tight cuffs and heavily embroidered designs. The intricate embroidery on the blouse, apron, and vest are usually sewn by a mother and daughter as a collaborative work of art.

The pleated skirt snaps in the front and the opening is covered by an embroidered apron. The color of the skirt is associated with the region, and Závadka *kroje* skirt colors are dusty rose, burgundy, or forest green. The thread on an original *kroj* is dyed with natural coloring such as berries or other vegetation; the use of water to clean the *kroj* is not desirable. In years past, the *kroje* were kept very clean while being worn for special occasions only, which included Mass. Skirts

James Kaliska of Phillips, Wisconsin, took his daughters to visit his ancestral village of Závadka in Slovakia. From left, the daughters shown in folk attire are Emily, Abigail, and Elizabeth.

made of a silky material are more conducive to pleating. The pleats are hand-sewn and the pleating operation requires heat.

The apron, of a white, light-weight cotton material, is usually embroidered. Peculiar to the region, it is pleated to a point at the bottom. The tie straps wrap around the waist twice, and tie in the back into a bow. Traditional care of *kroj* included an original antique *kroj* blouse not be ironed, as heat would yellow the hand woven, heavy linen type cloth. It was to be pressed cold using an old wooden boat filled with heavy stone that, when moved back and forth on rollers, pressed the *kroj* without the use of heat.

The *kroje* worn by males in the Kokava region served the needs of shepherds as they herded sheep to high elevations. The *kroj* shirt, intricately embroidered, was reminiscent of the women's blouse and the hand-stitched embroidery work was usually the work of the man's mother or wife. A heavy wool coat kept the chill off in the coolness of the mountain air. The coat was worn as a jacket, but oftentimes worn over one or both shoulders. A traditional wide, heavy leather belt held up slender wool pants. Wool was required to keep a man warm in the cool mountain air. While leather boots were most commonly worn, a ballet type sandal was also sometimes used in the region. Both woodsmen and shepherds wore green felt hats. Shepherds were usually also musicians and played a *fujara* to soothe their nervous sheep and wile away the hours in the quiet mountains.

Cornhusk shepherd doll playing musical instrument.

Sidonka Wadina: Slovak American Master Folk Artist

"You are the future.
It is up to you to pass this along so it will never be lost."

These words, spoken to me by my Slovak grandmother, Johanna Biksadski, marked the beginning of my career as a Slovak folk artist. I spent my early life listening to folk tales and stories of our beloved Slovakia while painstakingly decorating eggs with my grandmother for the Holiday Folk Fair, an ethnic festival my family has participated in for over sixty-five years.

In 1964, while visiting relatives in Slovakia, I was introduced to Slovakian straw weaving by my cousin, Vlasta. The beautiful spiral lantern she had woven was the first I had ever seen. I was so captivated by it that when she gave it to me, I immediately wished I could make one like that! At the time, I didn't realize that this ancient harvest talisman was traditionally created to wish upon, or that it would be the beginning of a lifelong fascination with straw and a wish come true.

—Sidonka Wadina

Sidonka, above, displayed her straw weavings at the Czechoslovak Genealogical Society International conference in Madison, Wisconsin.

Top left: *Detail of straw ornament*
© Spiral Heart

Below: *Detail of straw ornament*
© House Blessing

32

By the White House Christmas tree are First Lady Laura Bush with Sidonka Wadina, left, and daughter, Stefanie. Sidonka is wearing a vintage folk dress from Ábelová, Detva region. Stefanie is in a folk dress from Studienka, a village north of Bratislava and the place of her grandmother's birth. Previously by special invitation, Sidonka created a straw ornament for the White House tree, at the invitation of then-First Lady Hillary Clinton. The straw art, above left, is a Slovakian Marriage Piece, and at the right, is a Triple Heart. Both pieces are copyrighted by Sidonka.

Decorative Eggs

Decorative eggs have significant meaning in folklore and superstitious beliefs in Slovakia. Ancient custom suggests eggs symbolize fertility, life, eternity, joy, and friendship. Spring, sun, and warmth are also related to the creation and presentation of decorated Easter eggs.

Pin drop eggs at left are by Sidonka Wadina.

The eggs above, from the collection of Toni Brendel, came from relatives in Spišská Nová Ves and were done in the pin drop method used mostly in Eastern Slovakia.

Straw decorated goose eggs by Sidonka Wadina

Special Slovak American Events

Amanda Jane Ault, a Slovak girl, and former Miss Czech-Slovak State Queen, is shown at the International Holiday Folk Fair in West Allis, Wisconsin. Amanda is a folk dancer with the Veselica Slovak Folklore Ensemble in Chicago, Illinois.

With humble beginnings in 1944, the International Holiday Folk Fair has grown to become the nation's largest indoor cultural festival. The annual event, currently at Wisconsin State Fair Park in West Allis, is held the second full weekend of November. With over 60,000 spectators in attendance and over 60 ethnic groups involved, an aura of excitement, lively music, and dance permeates the atmosphere. Food in abundance is served by over 40 nations, each providing distinctive cuisine, and gift items from around the world draw early Christmas shoppers. The Slovak culture booth is one of approximately 30 that portrays the customs and traditions of its homeland.

Another annual event, but one which illuminates the Slovak heritage exclusively, is the fall festival held at the University of Pittsburgh in the Cathedral of Learning. Started in 1990, the Slovak Student Club sponsors the Pittsburgh Slovak Heritage Festival the first Sunday in November. Thousands enjoy Slovak entertainment, lectures, cuisine, shopping for Slovak imports and visiting vendors with related ethnic displays.

Modra Majolica Pottery

Nestled in the Small Carpathian Mountains of Slovakia, approximately thirty kilometers north of Bratislava, lies the village of Modra. At the edge of the village, a small, unsophisticated factory produces the country's most famous ceramics. Known as Slovenská Ľudová Majolika, the pottery techniques date back to the fourteenth century. During the sixteenth century, the Modra tradition was heavily influenced by Habáň craftsmen. The Habáňs were a religious sect that gained popularity during the Reformation and came into the area from Moravia, fleeing religious persecution. They brought with them this trade and, through assimilation, their techniques became dominant. They also introduced a more satisfactory technique of glazing the ceramics that proved to be more lasting and durable.

The traditional ceramics are graced with fine lines and colorful art work. Each piece is hand-spun, fired in a kiln, and whitewashed. The craftsmen then add their touches to the pieces in the painters' workshop. Floral patterns are the most popular today and they are painted free-hand. Some modern-day pieces reflect the grape motif, as the area is one of the larger producers of wine in Slovakia. In days past, various trades were depicted with tools of the trade painted on the surface of each piece.

The village of Modra has grown to 8,000 inhabitants. The factory now employs 25 artists and five potters, and is one of the last producers of this hand-crafted product in existence. A shop adjacent to the factory features a large display of Modra Majolica pieces for sale. Visitors are welcome to observe the production of this fine ceramics line by calling to schedule a visit.

Decorative Modra plates accent a family heirloom tablecloth.

Preserving The Slovak Heritage

Helene Baine Cincebeaux wears a flowered headdress from Liptovské Sliače in North Central Slovakia. Similar headdresses are worn by young women of that region before they are married. The headdress was made for Helene by a village woman. Once married, women wore heavy linen lace bonnets which looked somewhat like a flying nun hat. Helene often shares kroje *and other items for exhibition from her large collection of Slovak folk art.*

Many Americans of Slovak descent celebrate their Slovak heritage. Some have large collections of antique *kroje*, textiles, ceramics, and eggs created both in Slovakia and America by talented artists. New immigrants often joined or established dance and musical groups in cities from coast to coast, as well as in the southwest. They frequently perform at fairs, festivals, and America's leading tourist attractions, as well as in Slovakia. Special attention is given to performing historic folk dances representing various Slovak villages in authentic *kroje*.

The 50,000 Slovaks in Canada also preserve the memory of their homeland through folk dancing, poetry, and music. They are noted for sponsoring a Slovak Day in the Park for special celebrations.

Pottery by Mark Hudak

Potter/Artist Mark Hudak was born in 1954 in Chicago, Illinois. Slovak traditions and use of the language were kept alive in their home by his second generation Slovak parents.

Mark received his early education in Chicago area schools and later graduated from Concordia University in River Forest, Illinois. He pursued graduate studies at both the University of Washington and Pacific Lutheran University after teaching in a Tacoma, Washington school for several years.

Mark has created beautiful pottery professionally in the Pacific Northwest for almost twenty-five years. His strong sense of form and color are seen in his work, which includes a wide range of functional as well as decorative items. Even though Mark's work is highly controlled, an element of chance prevails as the glazes react to the way they are applied. This action intensifies each piece with exceptional radiance and beauty. While he makes reproductions of pieces of his

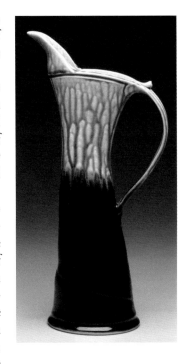

original designs, variations in glazes make each piece distinctive and unique. Mark produces his own line of dinnerware, sells at art fairs and galleries, and wholesales his artistic products under the name Stoneware Creations.

Mark Hudak's work includes a basket (left), platter (above), and a pitcher (above right).

Czech and Slovak Queens in Nebraska

This photograph of queen candidates and "little sisters" (younger girls who "shadow" the queens during national pageant events) was taken in Wilber, Nebraska, in 1998. Girls from many states compete. Lower left: 1998 Wisconsin State Queen, Allison Onchuck and her "little sister."

Above: *Megan Hoffman, (2002) Wisconsin State Princess.*

Slovak girl, Sarah Joy Nutt, of Phillips, Wisconsin. Miss Czech-Slovak Wisconsin State Queen of 2007–2008. Sarah attends Northwestern College in St. Paul, Minnesota.

Slovak American Folk Dancers

Veselica Slovak Folklore Ensemble

The Veselica Slovak Folklore Ensemble was founded in 1999 by Zuzana Fidríková in Chicago when Slovaks from several regions of Slovakia came together with the idea of preserving and presenting the traditions of their homeland through music and dance. Within the thriving troupe, several regions of Slovakia are represented. Each brings traditions and ideas from their respective villages to be shared, developed, and woven into Veselica performances. Musical Director, Pavel Melich, comes directly from Slovakia, where he was engaged in performing with various folk ensembles.

Moja Vlast˘ Folklórny Súbor (*My Homeland Folk Group*)
Czech-Slovak Dancers of Milwaukee, Wisconsin

This group has been in existence for over sixty-five years. The dancers pride themselves in presenting authentic choreography and folk dress that add color and drama to their dance performances. Directors of the folk group are a talented mother-daughter team, Sonka Šuvadová Tostrud and her daughter, Sonia Riečanová. Both are one-hundred percent Slovak and well versed in the traditions and culture of Slovakia. A native of Bystrička, Slovakia, the senior partner Sonka acquired a love for Slovak music and dance at an early age and instilled it in daughter Sonia, who began dancing as a child. Sonia was instrumental in introducing *Moja Vlast˘* as a student organization at Marquette University in 1997.

Moja Vlast˘ dancers in Slovakia

43

Tatra Slovak Dancers of Milwaukee

Originated in May 1972, their three groups of dancers range in age from five to forty-five years. Affiliated with the International Institute of Milwaukee, Wisconsin, the dancers pride themselves in having second and third generation members intent on keeping their heritage alive. Performances have been enjoyed by appreciative audiences all over America, in Canada, and in Slovakia.

Lucina Slovak Folk Ensemble

Since 1981, Lucina Slovak Folk Ensemble of Cleveland, Ohio, has been performing programs at international festivals and charitable events.

Members of the Lucina dance group are pictured at the Slovak Garden in Winter Park, Florida, U.S.A. In the Slovakian homeland, the ensemble performed in Detva, Východná, Martin, and many towns in southern and western Slovakia. The group promotes and hosts visiting dance groups from Slovakia.

Lipa Slovak Folk Dancers

Based in Minneapolis, the Lipa Slovak group, formed in 2001, performs primarily in the Midwest. Donald Pafko is the director and founder. They perform authentic, unchanged dances in authentic *kroje* from the Republic of Slovakia with all three regions of East, West, and Central Slovakia represented. Folk dress worn above are from the Šariš region and are authentic replicas of those worn by dancers performing at folk festivals in the Slovak Republic.

Left: Kristína Burgetová is from Bratislava, Slovakia. Her folk dress came from the Myjava region of Western Slovakia. This is an original, not replicated, folk dress.

Pittsburgh Area Slovak Folk Ensemble (PÁS)

Teaching their youth to appreciate the history and traditions of the Slovak people is just as important to the creators of the PÁS Folk Ensemble as the music and dance repertoires they teach. Celebrating the Slovak heritage through its re-creation has become a forte of this popular folk ensemble. Dedicated members meet once a week to learn every aspect of each music and dance program they perform. Performing on international stages and throughout the United States, the adult group shares vocal, instrumental, and dance expertise with younger eager dancers and singers as they promote interest in their heritage.

Once a year the members of PÁS *pose for a group photograph.*

Limbora Slovak Folk Ensemble of New York, Inc.

In 1966 a group of eight young dancers of Slovak nationality began dancing together. The small group was intent on upholding the traditions, music, and folk dances of Slovakia. Soon, over forty dancers, skilled musicians, and singers came together to enhance and honor the traditional music of Slovakia. Recipients of many awards and honors, Limbora received funding from the National Endowment for the Arts and the New York State Council of the Arts. Donning authentic replicas of original folk dress, with a repertoire of fifteen authentic folk dances, the group adds zest, color, and excitement to the program as they perform in the United States and abroad.

Rusyn Folk Dancers

Rusyns are a national minority in Slovakia, dispersed throughout the country due to job opportunities in Slovakia's larger cities. Rusyns speak an eastern Slavic language using the Cyrillic alphabet. Spiritually, they are either Greek (Byzantine), Catholic, or Orthodox. Rusyns, also, are minorities in Poland, Ukraine, Hungary, and Serbia. There are several Rusyn dance ensembles in America.

The Slavjane Folk Ensemble of McKees Rocks, Pennsylvania, preserves the cultural traditions of Rusyns through music, song, and dance. Slavjane has performed twice at the Rusyn Festival of Sport and Culture in Medzilaborce, in 1992 and in 2005, at the World Congress of Rusyns in Krynica, Poland, in 2005. They are shown above in front of the Orthodox Church of the Holy Spirit in Medzilaborce, Slovakia.

The Karpato-Rus' Ensemble of Cleveland, formed in 2006, promotes the culture and values of the Carpatho-Rusyn people in religious and folk traditions through dance, music, song, and skits. The ensemble has eleven members ranging in ages ten through fifteen. See photograph of the ensemble on page 190.

The Rusyny Folk Ensemble is hosted by St. Melany Byzantine Catholic Church in Tucson, Arizona. The twenty-five members specialize in Rusyn songs and dances from the Carpathian Mountains of Eastern Europe. The company was founded by Leslie Kurtak in 2001. Traditional choregraphy is by Dean and Jack Poloka. See photo on page 148.

Bratislava, The Capital City

Miro Pokorný, Jr. Day of Masters photography

In the precincts of the Bratislava Castle, overlooking the beautiful Danube River, the Centre of Folk Art Production annually presents traditional handicrafts and folk art, Slovak regional music, and the food of the Slovak people. On September 1-2, 2007 approximately 90 craftsmen took part in this annual event shown in the foreground above.

Creative workshops for children with hands-on experiences are offered and crafts people may enter in competitions. Master of Folk Art Production is conferred to the six best craftsmen selected at the fair. To date, 335 Slovak craftsmen and folk producers have been awarded. Through the combined efforts of ÚĽUV, Bratislava Culture Information Center, the Chancellery of National Assembly of Slovak Republic, and the City of Bratislava, with financial support from the Ministry of Culture of the Slovak Republic, this event is shared with the Slovak people.

ÚĽUV Dancers, Musicians, and *Kroje*

Left: Woman's kroj *from Ždiar*
Below: Fujara *player in Detva attire*
Right: Horn players from Makyta
Dancers from Podpolanie region

Dr. Martin Meša photographs

Dr. Martin Mešša photograph

Chief shepherds from Liptov

The National Museum for Slovaks

The National Czech & Slovak Museum & Library, located in Cedar Rapids, Iowa, is the only professional museum in the United States dedicated to the history and culture of the Slovaks and Czechs. The Museum hosts thousands of guests each year from around the world.

The Museum's 4,000 square-foot core exhibition, *Homelands: The Story of the Czech and Slovak People*, is a must-see for anyone interested in learning about Slovak or Czech heritage. *Homelands* takes visitors through one-thousand years of Slovak and Czech history and culture. The exhibit features exceptional examples of folk art, folk costumes, books, art, military artifacts, porcelain, crystal, and ceramics. Costume Square is a popular section that displays *kroje*, the folk dress from Slovakia, Bohemia, and Moravia. Twelve to fifteen *kroje* are on display at any given time, and are rotated regularly.

The NCSML is fortunate to own several leather coats from Slovakia that were made with the sheep wool on the inside and the tanned skin on the outside. The outside is decorated with appliquéd pieces of dyed leather. While women were usually the artists who embellished the beautiful textiles of Slovakia, the leather work was a man's art.

Sheepskin Coat: *The coat is made with the wool on the inside for warmth. Leather embellishment was usually done by men. Hundreds of tiny shapes cut from dyed leather have been appliquéd on the coat. An old legend predicts that if a newborn baby was placed on the furry side of such a coat, the child would have curly hair.* (On loan from the Helen and Robert Kindt collection)

53

The world-class museum collection includes nearly 10,000 artifacts and is constantly growing. The folk costume collection is the largest such collection outside the Slovak and Czech Republics. There are more than forty complete Slovak costumes from many villages and regions, including Piešťany, Ždiar, Heľpa, Trnava, Polomka, Myjava, and Čičmany.

Leather belt: *From Čičmany, Slovakia, the belt is from the 1980s. It is part of a man's* kroj *and is embellished with metal buckles.*
(Gift from John and Catherine Postemski 2004.22.50)

Folk costumes are not the only types of textiles in the collection. There are many fine examples of Slovak ritual cloths that were important in the momentous occasions of life. Christening shawls, wedding bed covers, wedding shawls, and birth cloths were beautifully embroidered with ancient patterns that held special meanings. Table linens and household textiles from Slovakia are also well represented in the collection. Of the hundreds of dolls in the collection, about half represent Slovak regions. In fact, many of the dolls wear *kroje* that are not represented in the folk costume collection, making them invaluable resources for the study and preservation of *kroje*.

Other artifacts from Slovakia include

Goldwork cap: *A piece of older embroidery dated 1875 has been integrated into an early twentieth-century bonnet.*
(Gift from Grinnell College in memory of the Steiner family 1993.27.8)

carved wooden cups, decorated eggs, sculpture, metal cookie molds, art work by Bratislava artist Ondrej Zimka, a *fujara,* the deep bass overtone fipple flute of Slovak shepherds, and a large collection of Modra pottery. A commercial sewing machine used by a Slovak immigrant who worked as a tailor in Pittsburgh, and a suit created by him, are among the highlights of the NCSML's Slovak holdings.

Two additional museum galleries offer a menu of exceptional exhibitions every year. Most exhibits focus on Old World themes. Notable exhibits with a Slovak emphasis have been: *The Tragedy of Slovak Jews,* which told the story of the Holocaust as it occurred in Slovakia; Works by Warhol that featured artwork by one of the most famous Slovak Americans, Andy Warhol of Rusyn descent; and Embellished Textiles: Absolutely Art, which featured embroidery, beadwork, lace, and other decorated textiles from Slovakia, as well as from Bohemia and Moravia.

Exhibits change often, drawing visitors back year after year. More than one hundred annual programs and events complement the Museum's exhibits. There is, literally, something for everyone to be found in workshops and classes focusing on traditional Slovak or Czech folk crafts, lectures by renowned scholars, concerts by world-class musicians, a national dance festival, films, conferences, cooking demonstrations, and even a reading society. Children love the annual Svätý Mikuláš Day puppet show in early December, and families delight in the annual Houby Days Festival in mid-May (organized by Czech Village). The

Beaded Vest from Orava Region: *The vest is black velvet embellished with thousands of glass beads. It was made in the early 1900s in the Orava Region of Northern Slovakia.* (Gift from Donald and Irene (Naxera) Hamous 1988.15)

Detail from wedding bed cover showing goddess motif

The color red is associated with fertility. The figure of the woman is called the goddess. This image dates back to prehistoric times and is thought to be a fertility symbol. Over time the figure has changed, and sometimes it looks more like a flower or a vase. The design has been passed down through the centuries, and the women who embroider it usually have no idea of its ancient roots.
(On loan from the Helen and Robert Kindt Collection.)

museum's twice-annual journal, titled *Slovo,* is also very popular. It is the only professional publication of its kind with articles by leading experts, written for scholars and laymen alike.

The National Czech & Slovak Museum & Library is truly a national museum. Its continuation and growth is an expression of pride for all Slovaks and Czechs, and signifies the importance of the Slovak and Czech culture to world culture. It is supported by donors and members from nearly all fifty states, governed by a board of directors and a national advisory board, and operated by a professional staff and 200-plus dedicated volunteers.

The National Czech & Slovak Museum & Library is a national treasure that must be visited in person to fully appreciate. Before your visit, check its website (www.ncsml.org) for the most current calendar of programs, information about current and future exhibitions, library information, and a link to the museum store online. Museum and library hours vary by season; closed on major holidays, and on Mondays in the winter. Call ahead or write to verify hours and admission. National Czech & Slovak Museum & Library, 30 16th Ave. SW, Cedar Rapids, Iowa 52404

Slovak Museums of Note

The Wisconsin Slovak Historical Society was founded in 1980 in Muskego, Wisconsin. Goals set forth by the society include recording and preserving the history of the Slovak culture in Wisconsin and continued celebration of Slovak traditions. An affiliate of the Wisconsin State Historical Society in Madison, Wisconsin, the organization became incorporated in 1980.

With a membership nearing one thousand, successful fund-raising efforts enabled the group to purchase a house for the museum, and heritage center at 3702 East Layton Avenue, Cudahy. Much of the large inventory of museum artifacts came directly from Slovakia. Donations from members of the society include *kroje* (national folk dress), farm implements, pottery, rugs, embroidery, lace, household goods, and books. Items given by fraternal lodges and many churches are also part of permanent displays in the museum.

Especially colorful exhibits are presented in open house activities during the Easter and Christmas holiday seasons. The two most important seasons of Slovak tradition are spotlighted with a vast array of traditional decorated eggs, wheat weavings, Christmas ornaments, and even holiday bakery.

A magazine, *Wisconsin Slovak*, is printed four times a year. For more information and to schedule appointments, write to: The Wisconsin Slovak Historical Society, PO Box 164, Cudahy, WI 53110.

Florida's Slovak Garden Library and Museum is in Winter Park, Florida. Founded in 1988 and referred to as the Slovak Archives, its main purpose is to raise an awareness of heritage in American Slovaks and to present all that the Slovakian homeland has to offer. Exhibits of Slovak literature, artifacts, and a complete collection of coins and stamps of the Slovak Republic from 1939 to 1945 are on site, along with a substantial display commemorating the life of the Father of the Slovak Nation, Andrej Hlinka. The Library and Museum are open to the public and a current schedule may be found at the Winter Park Chamber of Commerce.

The Jankola Library and Slovak Archive Center is located at St. Cyril's Academy in Danville, Pennsylvania. It houses a large collection of Slovak reference books which pertain to Slovak and Slavic history, language, literature, fine arts, spirituality and science. The collection also includes Slovak clothing, china, needlework, art, crystal, wood carvings, genealogy, newspapers, periodicals, rare Bibles and photographs. The library was named in honor of Father Matthew Jankola, Slovak immigrant priest, who promoted the education of children while preserving their faith and culture. The museum and library are open to the public and tended by the Sisters of St. Cyril and Methodius.

Paličková Čipka Bobbin Lace

Darinka Mojko Kohl, bobbin lace-maker, demonstrates at the Wisconsin Slovak Historical Museum, Cudahy.

As the founder and former owner of the Hook 'n Eye Costume Shop of Milwaukee, Wisconsin, Darinka Mojko Kohl cultivated an appreciation and interest in the beautiful handiwork produced by Slovak women.

Beautiful *kroje* were occasionally brought to her with requests for replication or repair. Many lovely pieces of antique embroidery, crocheted lace, tatting, and finer intricate laces moved through loving hands as she recognized the long and tedious hours of work that went into creating such finery. Darinka began collecting Slovak folk dress and soon realized that some of the lace edgings on the blouses and aprons were not all crocheted. She discovered bobbin lace. While attending a needlework conference, she found a bobbin lace kit for sale. The vendor offered assurances that she would be able to produce bobbin lace after a few simple lessons. She found that to be untrue.

Her interest piqued, she finally found a teacher in Columbia, and in Racine, Wisconsin. Darinka even went to France to a school for bobbin lace-making. While visiting in the Slovak Republic, she met women who not only made bobbin lace, but entered it in annual competitions.

She believes the making of bobbin lace is addictive, yet relaxing. Although not easy to learn, once the process is mastered a person can easily pick up on it after a long absence. With only two steps required in making the lace, one is soon producing it by the yard.

Today, bobbin lace creators have the advantage of good light and pillows on which to lay the work as the process moves along. Years ago, it was not that easy. In difficult conditions in the past, women created beautiful handmade laces, taking pride in their work. While traveling in Slovakia, Darinka discovered women who were able to make extra money while creating lace at home. As crocheting became popular, many women stopped making bobbin lace; it was easier to put a crochet hook and ball of thread into an apron pocket. They could then sit and crochet while tending animals in the fields. Now enjoying retirement, Darinka finds pleasure in creating doll clothes for her young granddaughters, and, on occasion, a bit of bobbin lace is added!

Slovak Fraternals for Families

Fraternal organizations and societies filled a need for newcomers to America. The practical needs of providing funeral expense funds and a small amount of cash to assist the family of a deceased were possibly surpassed by the sense of caring, belonging, sharing, and loyalty that folks experienced in their membership. With no welfare system in place, much of the dues collected was paid out locally to needy families in time of personal disaster. Social events amongst the immigrant members included card parties (at times the women stripped the down from goose feathers while the men played cards), dances, *divadloes* (theatrical plays at the Sokol Hall), and church-related activities.

As a child, I recall walking a few blocks to the Bartoš' home to pay the ZCBJ life insurance premium for our family. I'd come home with a receipt in my hand and we were good for another month. Západní Česká Bratrská Jednota (ZCBJ) did not stand for Zee Crazy Bohunk Jamboree, as one of my father's friends would have me believe as a child but actually translated to Western (region) Czech Brothers Unity. It later became known in English as Western Bohemian Fraternal Association and, today, as Western Fraternal Life Association.

Whereas the Association began as a Czech entity, it soon embraced Slovaks and eventually included all nationalities. There was such a large Czech and Slovak immigrant population in our area that there were five ZCBJ lodges, the earliest of which began in 1914. Joe Kuzma, WFLA State Director, remembers hearing of a time when an insurance "organizer" came by train from Cedar Rapids, Iowa, stayed at local homes, and signed up members for the new lodges. For each person signed he received one dollar. Mergers took place through the years and today there is a single active WFLA Lodge in the Phillips, Wisconsin, area. Its membership still administers to fellow members in time of need, and provides community service.

Friends Larry Vilda (a retired Nebraska director of WFLA) and John Fiala realized a dream when WFLA National President Phil Torticil, with encouragement from Joe Kuzma, endorsed the idea of WFLA becoming a major contributor to the annual Miss Czech-Slovak US Queen Pageant held each August in Wilber, Nebraska. As many as 23 states have been represented in a single pageant, sending young women of Czech, Moravian, Silesian, or Slovak lineage to compete for the crown. Substantial cash awards, scholarships, and paid travel to Czech and Slovak lands are awarded as prizes.

Although Western Fraternal Life Association welcomes people of all nationalities, the board of directors still honors the traditions embraced by its founders and continues to support this type of ethnic activity in America.

Pennsylvania

The largest population of Slovak immigrants congregated in Pennsylvania and a high concentration of Slovak Americans remains there today. The greater Pittsburgh area has 105,515 Slovak residents, giving metropolitan Pittsburgh the distinction of having the largest population of Slovaks in the world, outside of Slovakia. Slovak descendants continue to contribute to the American way of life with noteworthy strong work ethics, integrity, and firm family values.

No less than fifty Slovak fraternal societies were formed in the United States before the turn of the century and half of them were headquartered in Pennsylvania. Although first established to provide monetary compensation through death benefits, accident insurance claims, and to assist in times of illness, the societies took on another dimension, which provided social activities to its members. It was through this sense of community that many churches and Slovak language newspapers began.

Monthly meetings were held, dues paid, and, at times, even loans were made to members in crisis. The meetings began and ended with prayer. The ideals of American democracy were upheld; encouragement was provided to gain citizenship and the laws of the land were strictly enforced.

The Great Depression had an effect on fraternal organizations. Many people without work could not afford to pay dues nor help themselves, let alone help each other. That, coupled with the advent of President Roosevelt's New Deal, when social services became available, sealed the fate of fraternal organizations. Their reason for being was no longer necessary. Other social organizations, school, and church activities, and the prominence of movies and television, eliminated the need for the social functions of the lodges.

Today, the majority of fraternal organizations surviving in the United States are still in Pennsylvania. Within its membership, the sense of loyalty and support engrained in those early day fraternalists is still very evident. They continue to carry on the early ideals of their founders in the same benevolent spirit.

All of the registered Slovak fraternal benefits societies in the USA sponsor the Western Pennsylvania Slovak Cultural Association and each has a representative seated on the WPSCA board of directors. Those registered fraternal societies are: National Slovak Society, Ladies Pennsylvania Slovak Catholic Union, First Catholic Slovak Union of U. S. and Canada (Jednota), First Catholic Slovak Ladies Association, Slovak Catholic Sokol, and the Slovak Gymnastic Union Sokol of the USA.

The Cathedral of Learning

The Cathedral of Learning towers over the University of Pittsburgh campus and is recognized as the second tallest education building in the world. A historic landmark, the gothic structure was begun in 1926 and dedicated in 1937, but actually completed in 1939. Building construction was covered by contributions from many countries of the world, as well as local donors and even small school children who were encouraged to bring a dime to buy a brick during a time when fundraising was difficult and money scarce. Groups from many ethnic backgrounds share their pride in the magnificent nationality classrooms found on the first floor of the building. Groups designed and built a room in unique architectural style to reflect the culture and history of their countries.

One among numerous academic departments, the Department of Slavic Languages and Literatures is housed in the Cathedral, along with the Slovak Studies Program. The Slovak Studies Program is the only one of its kind in the U.S.A. Five Slovak American fraternal insurance organizations provide support

The Czechoslovak Room, above, which is used as a classroom, was completed in 1939. The ceiling of the room is a hand-carved, painted replica of a mountain villa in the Tatra mountains of Slovakia. Flowers indigenous to the Tatra region are painted on the beams. Frescoes on the walls are of famous Slovaks: Bishop Moyzes, Ján Kollár, Ľudovít Štúr, Cyril, and Methodius.

for an endowment that funds a full-time professor of Slovak language and culture. Beginning, intermediate, and advanced Slovak language is taught along with Slovak literature, history, and cinema through the program. The Slovak Heritage Festival is celebrated annually in the main hall of the Cathedral on the first Sunday of November. Visiting artists direct from Slovakia, cultural and historical exhibits, vendors, lectures, musical performances, and folk dancing are enjoyed by appreciative audiences.

The highest concentration of Slovak Americans in the United States remains in Pennsylvania and the Cathedral of Learning continues to be a vibrant, thriving hub of Slovak activity.

The Journeys of Joseph and Anna

An immigrant story: from a village in Slovakia to the coal mines of Pennsylvania, Ohio, and Illinois, to a farm in Northern Wisconsin.

Joseph Mráz was born in 1874, in the small, remote village of Nová Hutňa. Although he was born of Slovak parents, at that time the country was part of the Austro-Hungarian Empire. All subjects in what had been Slovakia were considered Hungarians.

In his boyhood, Joseph learned the carpentry trade and also gained proficiency in weaving willow baskets. These two talents were developed and used to great advantage in later years.

It's been told that Joseph just "happened" into the village of Iliašovce, where he met young Anna Brošková. Anna was born to Ján and Anna (Strauch) Brošková in 1880.

Although Joseph had the skills of a carpenter, he worked as a miner in the small mining town of Spišská Nová Ves. The land, rich in copper, iron, and silver had a strong tradition of iron ore mining that dated back to the fourteenth century, but mining was hard and dangerous, and wages were low.

An arrangement was made with Anna's parents. The two were wed in Spišská Nová Ves. They lived in Iliašovce where their first son, Joseph Jr. was born in 1898.

Since the middle of the eighteenth century, all male citizens between the ages of seventeen and forty under Austro-Hungarian rule were subject to compulsory military service. Under Empress Maria Theresa, military service lasted between seven and fourteen years. Once men entered, they remained in the reserves their entire lives. This produced hardship for their families.

In 1868, Austro-Hungarian military law instituted twelve years of military service. This meant three years in the army, seven years in the reserve, and two years in the home guard (militia, territorial army). The oldest son of a farmer was exempted from military service until the end of the nineteenth century, but that did not include Joseph.

If leaving the country, young men were often given a temporary passport, usually of one year's duration, to ensure their return to carry out military obligations. With these constraints, as well as poverty, religious persecution, and news that America promised a bright future, it is no wonder many young men left the country in search of a free life.

Faced with an uncertain future, late in September 1898, Joseph left his family and sailed to America. His plan, as it was for so many, was to find employment, save enough money, and send for his family. With friends awaiting his arrival in Pennsylvania, he readily found work in a coal mine in McKeesport.

Before the turn of the century, Anna and her son joined Joseph in America. She came well-equipped to meet the challenges of the new land. She was a hard worker and had good management skills. These qualities weighed heavily in the survival of the small family as they made their way in a strange land.

The most favored route for travel was through Hamburg or Bremen, Germany. The Bremen route was chosen by the Mráz family as they traveled to their new home in America.

Joseph moved his family from mining town to mining town, always looking for better conditions and a higher wage. Movement of the family is traceable according to each child's birth record: Anna, 1903, Youngstown, Ohio; Andrew, 1904, McKeesport, Pennsylvania; Margaret, 1906, Gilchrist, Illinois; Velma, 1909, Farmington, Illinois; John Bill, 1911, and Emma, 1916, both in West Frankfort, Illinois.

Anna was concerned about the unhealthy mining environment and dangerous underground labor. She lived in dread of the frequent reports of fresh mine cave-ins.

The moves from state to state also became a source of vexation. After the birth of their eighth child, Anna insisted they settle in one place so the children could be properly schooled. A permanent home was soon established.

The first of several tragedies struck the Mráz family when infant daughter Josephine died of pneumonia at the age of seven months. At that time, Joseph, Sr. began corresponding with a friend he knew from Europe. John Bandy settled in northern Wisconsin and reported that land adjacent to his was available. Forests were being logged out in that part of the country and lumber boomtowns were located along the North Central Railroad, all the way up to Canada. Bandy himself had settled his family in Lugerville, Wisconsin, near a large lumber mill owned by the West Lumber Company. The company town was eleven miles northwest of the city of Phillips, Wisconsin. The surrounding woods had been heavily timbered with virgin hardwoods, hemlock, and pine, and the flourishing mill stood like a sentry against the beautiful Flambeau River.

The lumber company provided housing for those who needed it. The company also boasted a general store, post office, barber shop, icehouse, saloon, and pool hall. Surely there would be work for Joseph and his young sons.

It took Joseph a week by rail to make the trip from West Frankfort, Illinois, to Phillips, Wisconsin. His friend awaited him. They traveled the fourteen miles to Bandy's farm by horse and wagon over bumpy corduroy roads. Early roadbeds were just wide enough for a wagon and team of horses. Perched next to Bandy, Joseph could see the washboard ripple that lay ahead.

The morning after his journey, Joseph examined the acreage next to the Bandy farm. On April 21, 1917, he purchased eighty acres of land from the Bohemian-American Land & Loan Company of Phillips for $700. The biggest selling point of the land was fifteen acres of tamarack swamp at the bottom of a hillside. This land reminded him of the terrain in his home country. The land also had numerous popple trees and white pine stumps, the remains of cuts made by West Lumber Company loggers.

With the purchase of the land, Joseph returned to West Frankfort to tell his family of his purchase. For the remainder of that year, he picked coal with his oldest son working alongside him. The two saved as much money as possible so they could make the move to the northland. Anna washed clothes for other miners, and that money was also tucked away. Andrew's paper route put additional funds into the family coffers.

By the following spring, Joseph had enough money for a team of horses, wagon, walking plow, cross cut saws, axes, and chains with grab hooks. Joseph Sr., Joseph Jr., and an adventurous eight-year-old, Johnny, made the trip together. Andrew stayed in Illinois to help his "ma," as did the rest of the family.

Mr. Bandy proved to be a wonderful friend. Work began on the roadway from Bandy's place, a good half mile, to what would be the Mráz farm. The Bandy women fed the three and put them up until their own shelter was built. The men worked beside them as often as they could take time away from their own work.

The first night in their newly-built shelter, as the men attempted sleep, a howling pack of timber wolves circled as though chastising the intruders. This was especially exciting to Johnny as it sometimes seemed the animals were right alongside him. Before long, exhaustion took hold, sleep came easier and they grew accustomed to the sounds of the northwoods. Later, Anna was to describe the location of their new home as "where the wolves say goodnight."

By September, the road was brushed out and ready for travel. Enough firewood was gathered, cut, and piled to last for two years. A clearing was made where the house would be built. The following year, some of the tamaracks would be cut to build the foundation for the house. Fortunately, a beautiful natural water spring was discovered about three hundred yards down the hill from the home site. This was used for water for five to six years before a permanent well was dug.

Johnny worked like a man next to his dad and brother. He wasn't happy when it was time to return to West Frankfort for school. With mixed emotions, they left their Wisconsin land and headed back to Illinois.

The next spring, Joseph Sr., Joe Jr., Andrew, and Johnny headed back to what they now referred to as the "home place." Joe got a job at the lumber mill and each day walked four miles to work and back. The others began building the house. They lived in the shelter made the year before until the house was roughed in. Joe Jr. bought all of the lumber needed for the structure and out-buildings through West Lumber Company. By late August, the house was pretty well finished.

Johnny and his dad traveled back to West Frankfort one more time. At last, all their possessions were loaded into a railroad boxcar. Anna had harvested vegetables and fruits from the garden in Illinois in anticipation of a long Wisconsin winter. Hundreds of jars of canned goods, along with furniture, clothing, supplies, and the family cow, made the trip. Amidst tearful goodbyes to friends and neighbors, they began their journey to Lugerville and a new life.

By the time the Mráz family moved to Wisconsin, young Anna was working as a domestic in a suburb of Chicago. She was employed by a Dr. and Mrs. Eastman. Her job was to care for their children and perform household chores. For the first time in her young life, she had a room of her own.

In accordance with Slovak tradition, Joseph and Anna arranged young Anna's marriage to Andrew Hudák in 1919 in West Frankfort. Her own life took on a new dimension apart from the family, even though she was not quite sixteen.

The first winter in Wisconsin was severe. The wind blew drifts so high it was impossible to get to town for supplies. Many times, the men stayed overnight at the boarding house in Lugerville, as the storms made roadways impassable and travel hazardous.

Life in the company town of Lugerville was simple. Although the settlement was self-contained, the town of Phillips was the place to go when needing larger items. A company general store supplied the needs of most. Clothing, shoes, household and hunting supplies, and groceries were available most of the time. Kerosene for the lamps was available, as well as gasoline and oil, as long as you brought your own quart jar.

Early one January day in 1920, as Anna looked out her kitchen window, she saw the company doctor hurrying across snow-packed fields. She immediately sensed something was wrong. Young Andrew had been killed at the saw mill. His clothing got caught, and he was drawn into a large running saw. As custom dictated, Andrew's body was laid out in a pine coffin in the Mráz parlor. Friends and neighbors came to pay last respects and offer condolences to the grieving family. During long winter nights, after the children were in bed, Anna and Joseph sat by the fire and wondered aloud if they had done the right thing in coming to Wisconsin.

Spring came and Anna stood with hands on broad hips, surveying the land. The first item of business was to cultivate a garden. Working together, the family plotted a strip of land two hundred feet long and seventy feet wide and began to plan and plant for the year ahead.

By most standards, the Mráz family was poor, but they never knew a hungry day. Anna knew they had to store food enough for six months of winter. Joseph Sr. and his boys hunted and fished; there usually was meat for the table. This included wild rabbits, partridge, ducks, venison, and pork. Their many chickens produced eggs, as well as additional meat. They had plenty of milk, cream, butter, and cottage cheese. Every summer a huge garden was planted, and as the vegetables were harvested, Anna and the girls began preserving them in glass jars. Each autumn the root cellar was full of hundreds of jars lined up on shelves Joseph had built for Anna. Row after row contained jars of beets, carrots, string beans, pickles, peas, apples, raspberries, and blueberries. They canned

66

Haying, like so many other farm chores, was a family affair. John and Emma Mráz are standing on top with Joseph and Anna (Brošková) Mráz below.

and smoked meats and made sausage. In one corner of the cellar, in large wooden bins, there were enough potatoes and onions to last the winter. Carrots had a separate bin and were buried in sand. They stayed fresh and crisp over the long winter months.

The entire family hunted for *hubas* (mushrooms) in the woods. These were strung with a threaded needle and hung to dry. Some of the mushrooms were pickled and some canned. Anna sautéed onions in butter, added mushrooms and caraway seed with scrambled eggs, for a special treat for her family. Caraway rye bread was a complement to this meal. They looked on it as a very special treat.

For several years, Joseph planted large fields of potatoes. Three years running he rented a box car and took potatoes to West Frankfort to sell. When there was an overabundance of vegetables, eggs, and milk products, Anna sold them in town.

The children attended Luger Crossing School. They walked and, when summer came, they often went to school without shoes. Shoes were saved, whenever possible, for Sunday. When one child outgrew them, the shoes were passed on to the sibling who best fit into them.

One late summer day, all but Anna went to the field to harvest poppy seed. Well into their labor, the children heard a shrill calling from the direction of the farm. Black smoke was unfurling skyward, and they began to run, knowing their home was burning. When they arrived, Anna stood helplessly by with empty buckets. She tried to put the fire out, but it moved too swiftly. The others ran for more water, but it was fruitless. Neighbors came when they saw the smoke, but nothing could be saved. Later, neighbors brought clothing, food, and offered to help in any way they could.

Next day, the children stood peering into the dark pit that had been their root cellar. There was nothing left but molten glass in clumps and clusters, with charred food remains under and about. The winter store of food was gone, along with their home. Precious photographs, legal records, and all of their modest possessions were gone. The hand-hewn wooden furniture Joseph carved out for his family had simply added fuel to the blaze.

The family slept in the barn's hayloft and began the work of reconstructing their lives. Before the snow fell again, another shelter was built.

In 1921, Joseph Jr. married Nettie Bejcek. They moved to Chicago to begin their life together.

In spite of hardship and pain, the Mráz family felt life was good. There were happy times along with struggles. One such occasion was the wedding of Margaret and Joseph Maleček. Margaret had gone to Chicago to work as a domestic. While there, she met Joseph Maleček, and she said it was "love at first sight." He came home to meet her folks and, in due time, the entire family found themselves deeply engrossed in preparing for the nuptial event. Joseph Sr. worked several days constructing a large wooden platform for the dance. Anna worked for weeks baking and storing foods. A good stock of moonshine, made by Joseph himself, was also in store. A small band of musicians was hired and, in the summer of 1924, an old-fashioned Slovak wedding took place with lots of food, drinks, and music – traditional Slovak fare.

Mother Anna had been ailing for some time. The family insisted she go to Chicago for medical attention. Since both Anna and Velma worked for Dr. Eastman, they believed he could help her. She made the train trip to the city and was diagnosed with colon cancer. It was in an advanced stage, and she died on the operating table. Her death in January 1929, at the age of 49, was a devastating blow to the entire family. She was buried at Lakeside Cemetery in Phillips, Wisconsin.

At the time, Velma was living and working with the Eastman family. On her day off, some friends took her to a dance where many young people from northern Wisconsin congregated. She met Charles Brendel of Phillips, and he asked her to dance. They were married in June 1929 in Crown Point, Indiana, and returned to Phillips, where Charles worked in the family business with his dad, a Czech immigrant.

By spring of 1931, the big timber had been cut from the land surrounding Lugerville and most of northern Wisconsin. With the great white pine decimated, there wasn't cause for the mill to remain open and it closed in 1933. People found it necessary to move to larger cities to find work, and the exodus from Lugerville began.

Life was never the same for the Mráz family after Anna's death. It seemed she was the glue that held them together. John and Emma were still living at home at the time, so it was most difficult for them. The older children had already gone their own ways. Emma soon went to Chicago to find work. There she met Atillio DeFabio and was welcomed into his warm Italian family. She married "Tillie" in 1935.

Joseph Sr. tried running the farm with the help of John, but found it too difficult. He moved to Chicago to live with his eldest son, Joe, and wife Nettie, and resided with them until his death at 66 in November of 1940.

The time came when a decision had to be made about the farm. For the last time, the two brothers stood in the yard by the farm house. With the farm sold, a sad farewell was said by the brothers, and each went his separate way. John had $39 in his hip pocket and owned a second-hand model A Ford. He was working in a Civilian Conservation Corps Camp at the time of the farm sale. He headed the old car toward the site and made a side trip to Soperton, Wisconsin, where a young woman named Esther was waiting. They were married in 1939.

Through the years, there were many Mráz family reunions. The surviving siblings were happy to be together. They shared memories, laughter, and tears, as they recalled the journeys of Joseph and Anna and the days that had belonged to all of them.

In our family, the name Jozef was always spelled Joseph, the English rather than Slovakian spelling.

The Mráz family was quite proud of its truck, a TT Ford, circa 1920s. John Mráz sits in the cab while Emma Mráz stands in front.

Annie

Annie (Kočí) Peroutka was our neighbor and of Slavic background. She became my mother's cherished friend, and the families lived as neighbors for over six decades.

A large, heavily producing garden meant much work in the harvesting. With a loud knock on the back door, before one managed to say "come in," Annie appeared in the kitchen more often than not, wielding a small paring knife. An accepted member of the family, she came prepared to peel, pare, clean, or otherwise assist in whatever kitchen chore we were involved in at the time. After a short amount of time spent working, mother brought water to boil, and everyone enjoyed a cup of tea, usually accompanied by fresh bakery.

Annie's arrival was always looked on with pleasure. She never sat idly during her visits, but helped with any chore at hand. She truly was a beloved character, not because the work was divided but because her presence was like comfort food for the soul. Mother and Annie exchanged many recipes and much food talk. If either baked cookies, usually a plate of them appeared on both tables, even in lean years. Likewise, jams, jellies, fresh vegetables, and other bakery goods were shared.

Annie served as chief neighborhood lifeguard, often herding a substantial group of small children across the highway, through Bloom's field, over Soo Line Railroad tracks, safely to the swimming hole in Lake DuRoy. After a few hours, we were ushered back again with safe home deliverance. This afforded our own mother uninterrupted sewing, which she did to bring extra money into the household. While summer fun was focused on Lake DuRoy and the green, small town landscape, winter pastimes included snowy outdoor fun and evening and weekend sessions of board games, with Annie presiding. Spending "time" was a beautiful example of making children feel special.

Not confined to kitchen activities, Annie and Mother partnered in sewing fourteen quilts that were raffled off as fundraisers for the Phillips Czechoslovakian Community Festival in Phillips, Wisconsin. For as many years, hundreds of winter hours were spent chatting and updating each other on family matters. They exchanged knitting and crocheting patterns on a regular basis, often crocheting the same doily patterns for their children and grandchildren, comparing progress notes as they went along.

Both women enjoyed playing contract bridge and, for many years, belonged to the same bridge club. Both widowed, they lived to see ninety-plus years and shared in celebration of each other's ninetieth birthday party.

*Annie (Kočí) Peroutka (left), and Velma Mráz Brendel (right),
both first-generation children of European immigrants.*

In today's world, special, enduring friendships such as the one enjoyed by Annie and my mother are rare. Long lasting, treasured friendships aren't the norm in the twenty-first century, in a time when families are transient and ethnicity watered down. More than being neighbors, in addition to their friendship, these women were first generation children of European immigrants. Their shared ethnic roots and the culture of their parents' Slavic lands provided a lasting bond between them.

Drawing by Sarah Krueger

Slovak Wedding Traditions

In my grandmother's time, it was customary for Slovak girls to be matched with a mate by their parents. This arrangement sometimes worked out, and sometimes did not. If not, it could be a miserable existence. The old adage, "You made your bed, now sleep in it" was often the case, even though they weren't actually responsible for making their own beds. In time, it was expected that love would grow between partners. If a common bond of respect and regard was present, this did happen. Perhaps a little luck came into play as well, and those marriages endured. Divorce was not popular, nor acceptable in that day, but sometimes necessary for the well being of those involved. Sometimes women stayed because they believed there was no place to go, and no other way. Likewise, the men.

At times, if so inclined, it wasn't unseemly for a boy to court his love interest by singing under her window. An invitation to enter by one of the girl's parents ensured food and refreshments would be served. Conversation and visiting took place, and the young ones were left alone for a respectable amount of time. When one of the parents reappeared, the suitor departed, on cue.

Once the wedding date was set, godmothers, relatives, and friends began preparing for the big event. There was usually a bridal shower that brought necessary supplies and equipment for the bride's kitchen and household. A relative or members of the wedding party usually sponsored a shower and felt honored to do so.

With a wedding day fixed, invitations went by word of mouth around the community. There were no formal written invitations. Letters had to be sent to relatives who lived a distance away so they could plan to attend, if possible.

Relatives and friends began preparing food. Hogs were slaughtered, hams smoked, sausages made, and pastries baked, all in a timely fashion, and brought to the bride's home shortly before the wedding day. Kolaches, *listy, rohlíky*, cakes and breads, the likes of which are only dreamed of, were stored up for expected multitudinous consumption.

The wedding gown was usually fashioned and sewn by a local seamstress. Many young women were taught the art of dressmaking as a vocation before leaving Europe and established themselves as seamstresses in America. In traditional white, the dress was usually heavily-embroidered and made of the finest material available. The richer, the finer; and that depended upon the bride's parents' ability to pay.

The wedding ensemble usually included a lovely headdress designed as one of a kind. This was a carry-over from Slovak village tradition and is evident in old wedding photographs. Seemingly, no two are alike. The headdress had a very significant place in Slovak tradition; a ceremony centered on it before the close of a wedding day.

Preparing the bride for the wedding was a duty enjoyed by the bridesmaids. Traditionally, before a Slovak bride left for the ceremony, she knelt in prayer in her parents' home and thanked them for their care in raising her, asking for forgiveness of any wrongs she may have committed along the way. There are many renditions of this prayer, and certainly each individual personalized it to fit her situation. The general prayer was to thank the dear mother who reared her in spite of many personal sacrifices and express sorrow at leaving her. The groom expressed similar thanks, praise, and regret to his parents.

In Slovakia, a horse-drawn wagon was decorated for the wedding party. If the groom lived in a neighboring village or some distance, he rode in the decorated wagon to meet his bride. He traveled with musicians who played lively music along the way.

Traditionally there were rituals and humorous goings-on. Upon the groom's arrival, the gate at the home of the bride's parents would be locked, and the groom would have to demand admittance. All was done with great drama and clarity. He would then demand his bride be turned over to him. Several bogus brides were sent out to greet him, masked and dressed in comical attire, only to be rejected as fakes by the prospective groom. With the shenanigans over, the bride appeared, and she and her groom either walked together or rode in the wagon, depending on distance. Along the way, well-wishers greeted the couple, teased, and gave advice. It has been said some stepped forward to hold up the couple, much like the "trick or treat" game played in America.

Finally, the ceremony took place, most usually at a church. (As time passed, many marriages were officiated by a Justice of the Peace, or a Judge.) If the ceremony was at church, tradition dictated the bride return to her home with her parents and the groom, the same. It was in the evening that they came together for a full celebration, usually at the home of the bride's parents. Again, the groom demanded his bride and was at this time readily accepted into the household, and his wife presented. A great feast and celebration followed late into the night.

After the banquet, one tradition included two bridesmaids taking their places on either side of the bride and groom to accept cash gifts in exchange for a sip of wine. With a large white linen handkerchief and a brush, a production was made of wiping the lips of the women who drank and giving men the "brush."

The most significant tradition had to do with the removal of the headdress or flower garland from the bride's head. With great ceremony, it was removed and a white cap or kerchief placed on her head. This signified she was no longer available, but a married woman with significant duties. From that point on she was referred to as a matron, and the head covering, or cap, was a *čepiec*. It covered all or most of her hair. Frequently, the bridesmaids sang songs during the "capping," usually quite melancholy, mourning the loss of girlhood. The older women sang songs of welcome, accepting the bride into their ranks. The groom, not to be overlooked, wore a hat adorned with flowers and a large plume. Although not a formal ceremony, the groom's feather was usually cut from his hat and it was said his feather was clipped. Marriage was a serious step and these rituals were very significant to the Slovak marriage ceremonies.

In some areas brides were "stolen" or "kidnapped." I witnessed this at several weddings, even as recent as a few years ago. Meant to be part of the merrymaking, some members of the male wedding party whisked the unsuspecting bride off to parts unknown. Usually the bride is taken to a tavern where a few drinks are served, more merrymaking takes place, and then the bride is returned to her groom. This is usually met with laughter and mocked disbelief, but is often part of the wedding celebration.

After the return of the bride, a bride's dance usually took place. I recall attending wedding dances at the local Sokol Hall. About mid-evening, the bandmaster would call for a "bride's dance." At that time men would take turns "cutting in" for a chance to dance with the bride. Each paid a fee to do so. The fee was collected by the Best Man or some other "officiant" and later given to the bride and groom to assist in starting their life together. This also was done with good-natured humor. It was a happy time. If the wedding dance was to end at midnight, about 11:00 p.m. sandwiches, placed in attractively wrapped boxes, would circulate around the hall. This was a welcome treat after dancing half the night, and a climax to the evening.

To escape the frolic and fun of the pranksters, the bride and groom had to make a quiet getaway. It was kept secret as to where their night would be spent. Otherwise, they were sure to become victims of more silly pranks. As it was, the married couple did not reach acceptable matrimonial status in the community until a shivaree took place at their home. This is defined as a noisy mock serenade. It usually took place a few days after the couple's return from their honeymoon and included loud banging on wash tubs, rattling of pans, and clanging pot lids in unharmonious clamor. Those closely related to the couple, either through friendship or relationship, took part in the shivaree. The group was invited into the house and lunch was served, usually along with a good wash of beer, sometimes homemade. After this ritual was performed, the couple was ready to settle in and begin their married life. To be shivareed was good because it was a sign of affection and acceptance. When the couple began their life together as man and wife, traditionally they lived with either the bride's parents or the groom's parents. It wasn't until the 1930s that some Slovaks broke away from this tradition. Before that time, it was the exception not the rule.

Oftentimes, the eldest son of a farmer inherited the farm, if there was one. In return, it was expected that a home would be built on the property for the parents, and they would live out their life under the care of the son. Such were the old Slovak ways.

A Slovak Wedding, 1924

The wedding of Margaret Mráz and Joseph Maleček in 1924. Left to right: flower girl, Emma Linduška (niece of groom); best man, Edward Maleček (brother of groom); maid of honor, Velma Mráz (sister of the bride); groom, Joseph Maleček; and bride, Margaret Maleček.

Margaret stood in the back doorway of her parents' home and recited a traditional Slovak prayer while her groom waited at the church in town.

> *My beloved parents: the time has come when I must leave you. The good you have done, and the pleasant life I enjoyed with you, makes this farewell very sad. I know that I received more than I deserved and can in no way repay you for these blessings.*
>
> *Although I am leaving, I will always be your daughter and will never forget you. For your love and goodness, I express my thanks. May God keep you in His care and guide you. I commend you to my Heavenly Father and wish you His blessings.*

Saturday was the customary day for weddings. The rural farm community had finished its work for the week and the entire neighborhood, encompassing many miles, had gathered for the long awaited event. Trinity Lutheran Church "on the hill" was the site of the nuptial vows. It was brimming over with well-wishers. Such an event was extra special and, in a small community, everyone came, as everyone was invited.

After the wedding, the folks went home to their farms to milk cows and do necessary daily chores. (There was a saying, "the cows won't wait.")

Dusk found them congregated at the bride's parents' home, where the social event of the season continued to unfold. The crowd arrived afoot, by wagon, horseback, and a few in autos. Anna Mráz had a reputation for good cooking, and the food fare was expected to be something to write home about. No one was disappointed.

Until midnight there was dancing and merrymaking. The family had prepared for the occasion for months. In Slovak tradition, a large wooden platform had been constructed—sturdy and large enough to accommodate all. The traditional music fare included polkas, czardas, and waltzes. The oomp-pah-pahs of the big tuba lured the oldest and youngest to tap their feet in rhythm. As midnight approached, the crowd became more quiet and serious. An air of expectation settled over them. At the designated time, as a new day dawned, a nervous bride stepped forward and took an elevated seat so all could see. She was indeed the center of attention. A green wreath, the symbol of purity and chastity, crowned her head. The matron of honor lifted the wreath from her head and another Slovak custom presented itself. Margaret sang in a sweet clear voice:

> *"Take off! Take off! Take off!*
> *My green flower wreath.*
> *Never will it, never will it be*
> *Placed again upon my head."*

A white cap was placed on her head by the young woman who attended her and Margaret accepted her life as the wife of Joseph Maleček. One more dance around the platform as the crowd pressed them, offering well wishes and light-hearted advice. Soon, the young couple made their hasty departure.

The last guest climbed up into his wagon and said, "dobrú noc and dobrý deň!" ("goodnight and good morning!") as Anna and Joseph Mráz surveyed their yard in the wee hours of the morning. They chuckled. Scattered around the yard were the remnants of the marriage celebration, and they knew the forest critters would have a party of their own. They would deal with the clean-up after a few hours' sleep. Arm in arm, they turned their backs on the stillness and walked into the house.

Epilogue

Joseph *(Pepik)* and *Teta* (aunt) Margaret bought a home in Stickney, Illinois. They had two children, Doris and Joseph Jr., and enjoyed a long, happy marriage. *Teta* Margaret found gratification in her life as a homemaker and stay-at-home mom and Uncle Pepik enjoyed his job as a steel worker. He walked high above the Chicago skyline on steel girders and delighted everyone in the family with (sometimes suspect) tales of his risky, adventurous work.

Journeys To Slovakia

Shortly after the founding of the Phillips Czechoslovakian Community Festival in 1984, the task was begun to record the histories of immigrant Czech and Slovak families in Price County. It precipitated an interest in my own family roots. My desire to be connected to my Slovak grandmother's people in Spišská Nová Ves (Slovakia), was keen.

In the early 1980s, my cousin, Dr. Ann Voda, gifted her mother Anna with a trip to our grandmother's homeland. Through the years, Ann's mother (my *Teta* Anna) had stayed in touch with her Aunt Mary (Brošková) in Ohio and received sporadic news of the Slovak family.

My first visit in 1987 resulted from the encouragement of my aunt and mother. With their guidance, I traveled to a distant land with little more than a list of names and some addresses.

Since my father had relatives in Vienna, Austria, I flew there, met his relatives, and rented a car. The Communist regime was in power. Crossing the border from Austria into "No Man's Land," filled with mine fields, to discover the presence of barbed wire fences, and soldiers armed with machine guns accompanied by police dogs, was both frightening and awesome.

My father's cousin, Dr. Frederike Kastenbauer, accompanied me with a rented foreign-made auto. One had the sensation of being watched. Thankfully, Frederike spoke some Slovak. On arriving in Spišská Nová Ves, I drove around looking for an address. When I saw an elderly couple sitting on their back steps, I stopped to get directions. When the name Broško was mentioned, the man hit his chest emphatically and announced, "Me, Broško!!" What are the chances?? We waited while Joseph Broško changed into a business suit and his wife a fresh dress, and then proceeded to the home of another cousin.

Contact with my relatives was limited and was confined to two of my mother's male cousins, the widow of another, and their families. One of the younger relatives, Mataj, spoke some English, and assisted with communication. I fell in love with the families and wanted to know them better. The second visit was similar, but more relatives surfaced, and after the "Velvet Revolution," subsequent visits revealed there were many more members of the Broško family yet to meet.

With freedom to move about, I was taken to cemeteries and different villages where I met or learned more about family members, past and present. With pride they showed us the churches, castles, museums, and beautiful Tatra Mountains. I felt welcome and accepted into their warm family circle. All of the homes of my Slovak family were well-cared-for dwellings with painted stucco exteriors. My mother's cousin, Emil, lived with his wife, Irena, in the home where my grandmother and her siblings, including Emil's father, were born. Emil was by profession a tailor, and conducted business in Levoča. He gave us a tour of his small shop and introduced us to some of the sights of the city. Many lovely Gothic structures dominate the city's architecture. A beautiful museum stands off from the town square almost across from Emil's shop.

One custom followed there, but not necessarily in the United States, is to take off your shoes when entering a home, whether you are a guest or resident. Most of our visits were centered in the home of Josefína, widow of my mother's late cousin, Štefan. Her home was quite large with an upper story. Josefína kept chickens and a garden. She had a long clothesline across the back yard, and frequently during our visits, clothes would be flying in the breeze. She and her daughter, Valéria, cooked many wonderful meals using their own fresh garden vegetables, along with pork chops, pork roasts, and chicken, roasted to perfection. Potatoes and cooked vegetables, rye and wheat breads, and desserts which included *koláčky* and fancy cookies were always enjoyed with a thick demitasse-type *káva* and a wash of *slivovica* (plum brandy)! Many special family occasions were celebrated in this home. Since the death of Josefína, the house is occupied by her son Petr and his family.

We also visited the home of Ivan and Mária Broško. Ivan was the son of my mother's late cousin Michal. Ivan worked as a railroad engineer and Mária was an elementary school teacher. Their son, Ivan Jr. is a professional basketball player. The younger son, Mataj, has completed studies at the university and is now in the work force. While at their home, Mataj translated for us between English and Slovak. A tour of their property gave us insight as to how people live in that part of the world. Ivan and Mária cultivated a small garden to provide fresh vegetables and fruit trees to provide fruit. A small shed houses a hog, raised to be butchered. A lovely flower garden and fencing provide boundaries between the neighboring lots. The walls and bookcases in their home were graced with items collected from far away places. Mária served a wonderful dinner one evening including *pirohy* with potato cheese filling and *pagáč* or *Kapustník* with cabbage.

I learned much from traveling to my grandparent's homeland. It was interesting to note that food I grew up knowing in America was prepared in much the same way in Europe. Soups were a daily tonic and vegetables were stewed or boiled. Meats were mostly roasted. Dumplings were in abundance along with potatoes. The main meal was usually eaten at noon, with soup as a first course. Tea was more popular than coffee, and bread was always on the table. Plenty of fresh raw vegetables made their way to the table and cooks were not shy in presenting baked desserts of the home-made variety. In Slovakia a bottle of *slivovica* is always handy.

All of the relatives seemed genuinely happy that we came to visit. Joseph, Emil, and Josefína are gone now, but the younger generation remains. Now I am a member of the "older generation" and must see to it that our traditions remain intact and are celebrated on both sides of the ocean.

Today, I am in touch with my mother's family and treasure all news of them. I've learned a little Slovak, and my cousins have learned some English. Communication gets easier as time goes by.

Although I plan to return to Slovakia sometime in the future, it is my fervent hope that my Broško cousins may one day visit the land their Anna Broško made her own over one hundred years ago.

Tatra Mountains drawing by Sarah Krueger

Growing Up The Slovak Way

Growing up in a Slovak household meant many things in my family, but the most vivid and warmest recollections are those centered around food preparation in our mother's kitchen. Mother was a multi-tasker before this expression became a buzz-word; she managed the household with aplomb. Nothing went wasted. Her creativity in the culinary arts presented itself unceasingly at our table. Otherwise quite staid, she was daring and innovative when it came to cooking. In her late eighties, she was still making full meals for father, trying new and modern ways of doing things—always cooking in the healthiest ways possible.

My three siblings and I were raised during and after the Depression, before and during World War II, and, after the war, during the Wonder Years of the 1950s. No matter what else was going on in the outside world, mother never flinched, shirked, or faltered when concocting nourishing and attractive meals.

Mother had three sisters and two sisters-in-law. These were five Slovak women, joined by one wonderful German Fräulein who married into the Slovak brood. Of the six, four wed Slovak men, one married a Czech, and one an Italian! Food fare was the common denominator. Conversations and recipe boxes were brimming over, seasoned with love and shared generously.

In four trips to our Slovak grandparents' land, I was privileged to meet the Broško family. Getting to know them during my travels to Iliašovce, Smižany, and Spišská Nová Ves, Slovakia, was sheer enjoyment. It was a bonus to discover similar dispositions: honest-to-goodness, down-to-earth openness that also prevailed in our American family. And, oh my, the food!

It brought me back to the fond early memories of kitchen-based family visits in the Brendel household. All of my aunts (addressed as *Teta*) pitched in and lent helping hands. I came to know it as the Slovak Way. Their steady chatter was lighthearted and laced with humor. It would bring all of them endless pleasure to know that their recipes are being passed on and shared with you.

Note: Recipe titles are given in English since most third-to fifth-generation Slovak Americans are not fluent in the Slovak language.

Wine bottle decoration with plaited straw by Sidonka

Slovak Table Grace

Thank you Lord God, Heavenly Father,
for every gift of daily bread.
Teach me always to receive it with
thanksgiving, for Jesus's sake. Amen.

Ďakujeme Pane Bože, náš všemohúci otec.
Za všetky dary a chlieb každý deň.
Nauč ma, aby som každý deň ďakoval
V mene Jezu Christa.

Beverages

Velma's Summertime Lemonade

8 fresh lemons
4 fresh oranges
2 cups sugar

Squeeze fresh lemons and oranges. Mix juice thoroughly with sugar to dissolve. Add water enough to fill a large pitcher and suit to taste. Add tray of ice cubes. Cut slices of orange and lemon to garnish glasses when serving. Add more sugar if desired. Mother served this from a big jewel tea pitcher. What a treat on a hot summer day!

Black Cow

> 1 large bottle root beer
> 1 quart vanilla ice cream

Put scoop of ice cream into large glass. Pour about 1/2 cup root beer over ice cream. Add another scoop of ice cream. Alternate ice cream and root beer until glass is full. Serve with a straw and long handled, iced tea spoon. Don't push the straw in too fast, or it will overflow.

Spiced Cider

> 1 gallon apple cider
> 1 can orange juice concentrate, undiluted
> 1/4 cup lemon juice, reconstituted
> 4 cinnamon sticks
> 2 teaspoons whole cloves
> 1 teaspoon whole allspice
> 2 cups water

Mix all ingredients in a large pan. Heat to boiling and reduce heat. Simmer for 45 minutes. Strain into metal bowl. May be served hot or cold. If hot, it is best to serve from the pan. Reheat to serve second helpings.

Christmas Eggnog - *Teta* Emma Mráz DeFabio

> 1/2 cup sugar
> 2 egg yolks, beaten
> 1/4 teaspoon salt
> 4 cups milk
> 2 egg whites
> 3 tablespoons sugar
> 1 teaspoon vanilla
> 1/2 cup brandy or rum liquor,
>   or 2 teaspoons of rum extract

Beat 1/2 cup sugar into egg yolks and beat well. Add salt. Stir in milk. Cook over hot water in double boiler, stirring constantly.

When mixture coats the spoon, cool. Beat egg whites until foamy, adding 3 tablespoons sugar. Beat to soft peak stage. Add to cooled custard and stir thoroughly. Chill for 4 hours or overnight. Pour into small punch bowl. Add mounds of whipped cream sprinkled with nutmeg. Makes 6 servings.

Appetizers

A typical Slovak meal is so hearty that appetizers are not usually served. These recipes are sometimes served as a pre-meal offering later in the afternoon with *slivovica* (plum brandy) or a glass of wine.

Here are several different suggestions for appetizers: equal parts of cooked tongue, calf's brain, and cooked spinach; ground fine, seasoned with garlic salt and moistened with mayonnaise. Served with melba toast. Sardines creamed with mayonnaise, grated onion, and lemon juice. Serve with melba toast.

Sheep cheese or goat cheese (sliced). Served with crackers.

Serve raw vegetables whenever in season.

Miniature Cream Puffs - *Teta* Anna Mráz

1 cup water
1 stick of butter
1/2 teaspoon sugar
1/4 teaspoon salt
1 cup flour
4 eggs

Measure water into a medium-sized saucepan. Cut butter stick into small pieces and add to pan. Heat until the butter melts. Add sugar and salt and remove from heat. Add flour while stirring constantly. Stir until all mixed in. Return to heat and continue stirring until large ball is formed. Put mixture into mixing bowl. Cool slightly. When cool, add eggs one at a time and keep stirring. Let mixture sit at room temperature for about an hour. Drop cream puff batter by heaping teaspoons onto a lightly greased cookie sheet.

Bake in preheated 425 degree oven for 10 minutes. Then reduce heat to 375 degrees and bake 15 minutes more. Reduce heat a third time to 325 and bake for 10 more minutes. Makes about 40 miniature cream puffs.

Cool and split open with a small knife. A variety of fillings may be used.

Chicken Liver Spread - *Teta* Anna Mráz

Serve as filling for cream puffs or in a bowl with small cocktail rye bread or crackers.

> 1 pound chicken livers
> 2 sticks butter, softened
> 1/4 cup grated onion
> 1 teaspoon dry mustard
> 1 teaspoon garlic salt

Wash and trim livers. Cook in water enough to cover. Simmer for 1/2 hour. Cool and drain. Grind chicken livers in grinder or food processor, adding soft butter. Blend in onions, dry mustard, and garlic salt.

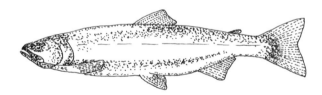

Smoked Salmon Filling

> 1/8 pound smoked salmon or smoked carp
> 8 ounces sieved cottage cheese
> 3 tablespoons milk
> 1/2 teaspoon black pepper, freshly ground
> 1/2 teaspoon onion salt

Debone smoked fish and add to sieved cottage cheese. Put fish mixture through the food grinder with the finest blade. Add milk and seasonings and blend well. Serve as filling for cream puffs, in bowl, or spread on cocktail rye or slices of cucumber.

Egg Salad Filling

    4 eggs, hard-boiled and diced
    1/2 cup mayonnaise or salad dressing
    1 tablespoon prepared mustard
    1/2 cup minced celery
    1/2 cup minced onion
    1/4 cup pickle relish or minced pickle

Mix thoroughly. Put a generous tablespoonful in each cream puff.

Šudlíky

I've never heard of another name for the snack my mother made called šudlíky. *I just don't know what it would be in English.*

    2 cups mashed potatoes, cooled
    2 large eggs, beaten
    Pinch of caraway seed
    2 cups sifted flour
    1/2 teaspoon salt
    2 tablespoons butter, melted
    1 teaspoon coarse salt

Add eggs to potatoes and mix thoroughly. Add caraway seed. Mix flour and salt and add to eggs and potatoes. Mix well. Turn mixture out on floured bread board. Roll out to about 1/4 inch thick. Cut short sticks (about 1-1/2 inches) and place on greased cookie sheet. Repeat using all dough. Bake in 350 degree oven 10–12 minutes. Cool. Dip in melted butter in skillet and brown over medium heat. Remove and roll in coarse salt. Serve immediately or let dry and serve later.

Deviled Eggs

1 dozen eggs, hard-boiled
3/4 cup mayonnaise or salad dressing
1 tablespoon prepared mustard
1 small onion, minced
1 stalk celery, minced
2 tablespoons minced sweet pickle or pickle relish
1/4 teaspoon garlic salt
1/4 teaspoon celery salt
2 drops yellow food coloring (optional)
Pimiento-stuffed olives (optional)

Do not overcook eggs or yolks will turn green. Once boiling, turn off heat and allow to sit in hot water for 15 minutes for small eggs, 18 minutes for larger eggs. Drain, cool and peel. Cut eggs in half and empty yolks into bowl. Arrange whites on a platter. Mash yolks and mix in mayonnaise or salad dressing, seasonings, and mustard. Add onions, celery, pickles. Add food coloring if yellow tint is desired. When mixed altogether, spoon into whites on platter. Sprinkle with paprika. Garnish with a slice of olive and pimiento. Cover and refrigerate until ready to serve.

Open-Face Sandwiches

1 loaf rye bread
1 loaf whole-wheat bread
1 loaf white bread
Fillings selected from appetizer recipes

Cut crusts from bread. Spread each piece of bread completely with filling, cut into triangles, squares, or strips OR use cookie cutters to make desired shapes and then frost with fillings. (Save excess pieces of bread from cookie cuts for bread crumbs.) Garnish with slice of olive, pickle or strip of pimento. Sprinkle with paprika before serving.

Soups

Every day was soup day as we had soup for at least one meal for as long as I remember. The big meal was eaten at noon, with soup usually for the evening meal. Mother really meant it when she said, "Soup's on!" We would usually scurry if we were within earshot! Before working in the kitchen, all cooks had to wash their hands thoroughly. "Cleanliness is next to Godliness" was an oft' repeated phrase!

My mother used a lot of butter, rather than oleo, and browned flour in it to add extra flavor to soups. She used the tops of celery in her soups, always. When she got older, I noted she did take some shortcuts and, for example, used pre-cooked rice.

Also, the butter and cream gave way to lowfat margarines and even skim milk! It never tasted the same, but was better for us.

Now, in the interest of good health, I use the lower calorie, lower cholesterol products. About once or twice a year I go all out and make the true recipes to treat my friends! The funny noise we hear while eating could possibly be our veins clogging up!

Liver Dumpling Soup

**2–3 pounds beef roast
   with bone, or soup meat
1 cup diced carrots
1 cup diced celery
1 cup diced onion
2 quarts water
Salt and pepper to taste**

Wipe beef bone and meat with damp cloth or rinse. Using large soup pot, cover soup meat with water. Cover and simmer for 2 hours, longer if meat is tough. Add more water if needed. When meat is tender, add carrots, celery, and onion to beef stock. Simmer for 20 more minutes. While soup is cooking, mix ingredients for liver dumplings. (See next page.)

Ingredients for Liver Dumplings

1/3–1/2 pound liver (calf liver is best)
1 egg, beaten
1/4 stick softened butter
2 cloves fresh garlic, minced
1/2 teaspoon salt
1 teaspoon marjoram
1/4 teaspoon mace
1/4 teaspoon ground pepper
1/4 teaspoon allspice
1 cup bread crumbs, more if mixture hard to handle

Preheat oven to 250 degrees. Remove meat from soup. Discard bone or treat the family dog! Put meat into oven to keep warm. Grind liver in meat grinder or food processor. In a deep bowl, add all ingredients and mix together using a wooden spoon. Bring soup stock to rolling boil. Wash hands and dry. Roll balls of liver mixture the size of a golf ball in the palms of your hands. Drop the dumplings into beef broth and reduce heat. Cook for 15 minutes. Serve from a soup tureen. Sprinkle minced fresh parsley over each bowl of soup before serving. Serve soup meat on platter, along with tomato gravy (see page 129) and bread dumplings (see page 162). Makes 6–8 generous servings.

Sauerkraut Soup

1 quart jar homemade sauerkraut
   or 1 large can sauerkraut (28 ounces)
1 quart water
1 large onion
1/4 stick butter (more, if needed)
1/4 teaspoon caraway seed
1 quart half-and-half (milk and cream), divided
2 heaping tablespoons flour
1/4 teaspoon each salt and pepper
2 eggs

Wash sauerkraut and let drain in colander. Dice onion and brown in butter. Set aside. Put sauerkraut into large pot and cover with water. Add browned onion and scrape fry pan with a food scraper. ("Waste not, want not.") Rinse pan and add to soup. Add caraway seed. Simmer for 1/2 hour.

While soup is cooking, pour 1/2 of the half-and-half into pint jar. Add flour and shake well. Set aside. Adding flour to liquid rather than adding liquid to flour reduces lumps. Add balance of half-and-half to soup. Bring almost to a boil.

When ready, stir in pint of liquid thickener you've made, stirring constantly. Again, bring almost to boil. Add salt and pepper to taste. Add 2 whole eggs and stir with wooden spoon so eggs separate and cook into small pieces. Do not boil, but keep almost boiling. When ready to serve, remove from heat. Serve from soup tureen. 6–8 generous servings.

Note: Some recipes call for eggs to be cooked whole in the liquid, but this is the way our family makes it.

Pork and String Bean Soup

> 2 quarts water
> 2–3 pounds of lean pork ribs
> 1 cup diced carrots
> 1 cup diced celery
> 1 cup diced onion
> 2 cans whole green string beans, drained
> 1 quart of half-and-half, divided
> 2 tablespoons flour
> 1/2 teaspoon salt
> 1/2 teaspoon pepper
> 1/4 teaspoon paprika

Cook ribs in water for 1 hour. Remove ribs and set aside. Cool broth in refrigerator until fat can be skimmed from the top. Reheat and add vegetables, except string beans, and cooked ribs. Bring broth to boil and cook about 20 minutes until vegetables are cooked but not over-done. Put 1/2 of the half-and-half in pint jar with 2 tablespoons flour to make a light thickening. Shake well until lumps disappear. Add to soup, stirring into liquid. Add remainder of half-and-half and string beans, and heat thoroughly. Serve in soup bowls and sprinkle with paprika. 6–8 servings.

Tomato Rice Soup with *Zápražka*

> 1 quart home-canned tomatoes or large can (28 ounces)
> 1 can water (28 ounces)
> 1 cup diced celery
> 1 cup diced onion
> 3/4 cup cooked, rinsed rice
> 1/4 teaspoon salt
> 1/4 teaspoon pepper

Simmer tomatoes, water, celery, and onion for 20 minutes until celery and onion are cooked, but not overdone. Add rice and heat thoroughly. Make *zápražka* to add to the soup.

Zápražka (Roux)

> 1/4 stick butter melted in small fry pan
> 2 tablespoons white flour
> 1/2 cup water

To make *zápražka*, add the flour, sprinkled a little at a time into the browning butter, stirring constantly. Add water. Stir. It will sizzle. Add browned flour mixture to soup, and stir. *Zápražka* gives added flavor to soups.

Chicken Rice Soup

> 1 whole chicken, cut up
> 2 quarts water
> 1 onion, diced
> 2 carrots, diced
> 2 celery stalks, with tops, diced
> 2 teaspoons chicken base
> 1 cup cooked rice, rinsed
> 1/2 cup chopped fresh parsley

Put washed, cut-up chicken in large pot. Cover with water and cook with lid on until fork tender. Remove chicken from stock and set aside. Wash and add vegetables. Celery tops give extra flavor and shouldn't be wasted. Cook for 20 minutes until tender. Skin and remove chicken from bone. Cut up chicken and put back into pot. Add chicken base for added flavor. Add cooked rice. It is rinsed so soup doesn't get cloudy. Add fresh parsley before serving. 6–8 servings.

Chicken Dumpling Soup

1 whole chicken
2 quarts water
1/4 teaspoon caraway seed
1 whole onion, diced
2–3 carrots, diced
2–3 stalks of celery with tops, diced
1/4 teaspoon salt
1/4 teaspoon pepper
1/2 cup fresh, chopped parsley
2 tablespoons chicken soup base or 2 bouillon cubes

Wash, cut up and cook chicken in water. Necks and wings give soup added flavor. Add caraway seed. Stew until fork tender. Remove chicken from broth with skimmer. Refrigerate broth and when cool, skim off fat. Reheat. Prepare and cook vegetables in broth for 10–15 minutes. Add parsley. When cool, bone and skin chicken as desired. Add to cooked vegetables and broth. Add chicken base or bouillon to taste. Salt and pepper to taste. Add soup dumplings.

Soup Dumplings

3 eggs
3 tablespoons water for hard dumpling, OR
   3 tablespoons milk for softer dumpling
1/2 teaspoon salt
Dash celery salt
2 scant cups flour (approximately)

Mix eggs with water or milk and blend well. Add seasonings and enough flour to make soft dough. Mix well with wooden spoon. If too sticky, add flour, if too stiff, add liquid. Turn dough out onto dinner plate for easier handling. Slide batter into any soup with tablespoon. Bring soup back to boil gently and close cover to cook. Keep temperature not too high or it will boil over. Cook dumplings 10–12 minutes. Drain and add to soup. Serves 6–8.

Red Kidney Beans and Ham Hocks

> 1 large package of dried red kidney beans
> 2 quarts water
> 1 small onion, cut up
> 2–3 smoked ham hocks
> 4–5 stalks celery, cut into 4 inch pieces
> 1/4 teaspoon fresh ground pepper
> Ham soup base (optional)

Wash red kidney beans, sort, and soak overnight in water. In the morning cover beans with water and cook 2 hours. Add onion. Rinse ham hocks and add to beans. Cook until beans are tender. Add celery cut about 4 inches in length. Simmer until celery is tender, about 15–20 more minutes. Add 2 tablespoons smoked ham soup base for extra flavor, if desired. Remove ham hocks from soup, cut up and serve on platter. Serve soup in bowls and pass the meat around. 6–8 servings.

Cabbage Soup

> 2 quarts water
> 1 quart home-canned tomatoes
>   or 1 large can tomatoes (28 ounces)
> 1/2 head cabbage cut into large pieces
> 3 large carrots, diced
> 3 large stalks celery, diced
> 1 large onion, diced
> Beef stock or ham base (optional)
> *Zápražka* (optional—see page 90)

Wash all vegetables, dice and simmer until vegetables are done to desired consistency. Add beef stock or smoked ham soup base for flavor. Add *Zápražka* for additional flavor. Makes 6–8 servings.

Slovak Onion Soup

1/2 stick sweet cream butter
2 large homegrown sweet onions, sliced in 1/8 inch slices
2 quarts water
2 tablespoons Worcestershire sauce
8 beef bouillon cubes
   or 2–3 tablespoons beef base
1/2 cup hot water
Rye bread toast
1/2 cup grated Parmesan or Swiss cheese

Melt butter in large pot and allow to brown tenderly. Add sliced onions. Continually stir with wooden spoon, but do not overcook! Add water and Worcestershire sauce. Bring to boil. Simmer gently. Dissolve bouillon cubes or beef soup base in measuring cup of hot water and add to soup mixture. Bring to boil. Let simmer a few minutes, but don't allow onions to cook until mushy. Toast rye bread and cut into cubes. Dish up soup and add bread cubes on top. Garnish with shredded Parmesan cheese or shredded Swiss cheese. Makes 6–8 servings.

Breads, Raised Dough, Dumplings & Noodles

Basic White Bread - *Teta* Nettie Bejček-Mráz

Teta Nettie advises, "In place of regular tap water, save potato water from last night's boiled potatoes. Your bread will be more moist."

> 2 packages dry yeast
> 2 cups warm water, divided
> 3 tablespoons sugar, divided
> 6 cups flour
> 2 teaspoons salt
> 1 cup warm milk
> 2 tablespoons lard or butter

Dissolve yeast in 1 cup of warm water along with 1 tablespoon sugar. Mix together flour, salt, 1 cup warm water, 1 cup milk, lard or butter, and 2 tablespoons sugar. Pour yeast mixture into flour mixture, stir, and knead 8 to 10 minutes. Allow to rise in greased bowl in a warm place, covered with a towel. After 1 hour, punch dough down. Divide into loaves, let rise again in bread pans for about 1 hour. Brush loaves with melted butter. Bake at 375 degrees 30–45 minutes or until golden brown. Yields 2 loaves.

A *Koláče* is a *Koláčky* is a Kolache....

One wonders why there are so many different spellings and pronunciations for the word *koláče*. It's because there are so many varieties and so many cooks who add their own "touches." The name *koláč* originated from its shape: *kulatý jako kolo*—round like a wheel. The basic *koláč* was a piece of raised dough made round and flat, about 8 to 10 inches in diameter. The center was pushed down and filled with fruit fillings, poppy seed, or cottage cheese. On special holidays, the *koláče* was made smaller and daintier, about 2-1/2 to 3 inches in diameter. This took more time and wasn't the usual practice, but women put more time into preparing for special occasions. In Western Slovakia, the people made small filled pockets about 2 to 3 inches square. They were filled with the usual traditional fillings. These were called *koláčky*. (*koláč*, plural: *koláče*, small *koláč—koláček*, plural: *koláčky*.) After baking, the hot top was painted lightly with beaten egg whites and sprinkled with powdered sugar.

Yes, there are many versions of the favorite, *koláčky*, and almost as many spellings for the word. Here is our favorite family *koláčky* recipe. *Koláčky* are served at all festive occasions including Christmas.

Koláčky

> 2 cups scalded milk
> 1/2 cup sweet butter
> 1/2 cup sugar
> Lemon rind from 1/2 lemon
> 2 egg yolks
>   (whites make a less refined dough)
> 1 cake of yeast dissolved in 1/4 cup warm water
>   (or 1 package of dry yeast)
> 1 teaspoon salt
> 6 cups flour, unsifted
>   (If sifted, add a more generous cup)

Scald milk; add butter, sugar, lemon rind, and egg yolks. Let cool to lukewarm. Add yeast, letting it work for 15 minutes. Add salt and flour. Mix well with wooden spoon. Let rise in warm place for at least 1 hour. Punch down. Roll on floured board to about 1/2 inch thickness. Cut into rounds. Use small juice glass. Let rise on greased cookie sheets for 1/2 hour. Using an index finger and the middle finger of both hands, make indentation in middle of *koláčky*. Fill with desired filling.

Don't let rise again after filling is in. Cover with streusel. Bake at 350 degrees for 20 minutes. Brush lightly with butter after removing from oven. Use a *pierko* (feather pastry brush) to brush butter. When finished using it, wash brush in hot soapy water, then rinse in hot water. Store for next time use!

An alternative for different shaped kolaches is to cut dough into squares instead of rounds. Turn out dough onto floured board and roll to about 1/2 inch thickness. Cut into about 3-inch squares. Stretch out corners and put filling in center. Take up corners crossways and pinch together in center.

Streusel Topping

    1 cup sugar
    1 cup shortening or margarine, melted
    2 cup flour
    2 teaspoon cinnamon (optional)

Mix ingredients together. Crumble, as for pie crust.

Prune Filling

    1 pound dried prunes
    Water to cover
    1/2 cup sugar
    1/2 teaspoon cinnamon

Cook 1 pound of dried prunes until soft. Cool. Drain. Remove pits and mash. Add sugar and cinnamon. Mix and spoon into *kolaches*.

Poppy Seed Filling One

    1 pound poppy seed, ground
    2 cups hot milk
    2 tablespoons grape jelly
    1 tablespoon brandy
    1 cup raisins
    1 cup sugar
    3 tablespoons butter or margarine

Grind poppy seed in poppy seed grinder. Empty into small pan. Add milk, jelly, brandy, and sugar. Cream until the mixture sticks together. Bring to boil. Cook while adding raisins. Stir constantly. Cook about 5 more minutes. Add butter. Remove from heat and cool.

Poppy Seed Filling Two

3 cups ground poppy seed
Milk to make desired consistency
3 tablespoons white syrup
3/4 cup sugar
1 teaspoon vanilla

Grind poppy seed in poppy seed grinder. Empty into small pan. Add milk, syrup, vanilla, and sugar. Cream until the mixture sticks together. Bring to boil. Stir constantly. Cook about 5 more minutes, then cool.

Nut Filling

2-1/2 pounds finely chopped walnuts
1-1/2 pounds powdered sugar
8 egg whites, beaten
1 teaspoon real vanilla
1 tablespoon cinnamon
1/2 cup white Karo® syrup

Mix all ingredients together. If necessary, add a bit of milk.

Cottage Cheese Filling

1 pound dry cottage cheese
1/2 cup sugar
2 egg yolks
1 teaspoon salt
1 tablespoon cornstarch
1/2 cup raisins
1/2 teaspoon mace
1/2 teaspoon cinnamon

Mix all ingredients together well for coffee cakes or *koláčky* filling. If dry cheese is not available, use creamed, but freeze first. Creamed cottage cheese can also be drained through sieve and used. Freezes well.

Sour Cream *Koláčky* - *Teta* Anna Mráz

    1 large cake yeast
    1/2 cup warm water
    8 cups flour
    3 teaspoons baking powder
    1 pound butter, softened
    1 pound oleo, softened
    1 pint sour cream
    8 egg yolks
    1/4 cup lukewarm milk
    Sugar for rolling
    Egg whites

Dissolve yeast in warm water. In large bowl sift flour and baking powder together. Add butter and oleo and mix together. Add sour cream, beaten egg yolks, and milk with yeast mixture. Mix thoroughly and refrigerate overnight. In the morning divide dough into 4 parts. Put small amount of sugar on bread board and roll dough out on sugar. Cut into 3-inch squares and put filling in center. Fold all four corners into middle and pinch. Repeat until all 4 parts of dough are used. Can also make these into crescent shapes with filling inside. Brush tops with beaten egg whites and bake for 15 minutes in 325 degree oven.

Sugar Doughnuts

    1 cup milk
    1 cake yeast
    3-1/2 cups flour, divided
    1/4 cup lard
    1 teaspoon salt
    2 teaspoons sugar
    1 egg
    1/4 teaspoon cinnamon, mixed with sugar

Heat milk, dissolve yeast in it. Add 1-1/2 cups of the flour and beat well. Cover and let rise till double in bulk. Cream lard, salt, and sugar, and add egg. Stir this into yeast mixture. Add remainder of flour and beat five minutes. Rub with lard and let rise until double in bulk. Punch dough down and put on floured board. Roll 1/2 inch thick. Cut doughnuts with cutter. Let rise once more and fry in deep fat until brown on both sides, tipping over with a wooden spoon. Remove from fat to brown paper, let drain and cool. Roll in granulated sugar to which cinnamon is added.

Cinnamon Rolls - *Teta* Emma Mráz-DeFabio

> 1/2 cup warm water
> 1 package dry yeast
> 3 tablespoons granulated sugar, divided
> 2/3 cup milk, scalded and cooled
> 1/4 cup melted butter
> 2 eggs
> 1/2 teaspoon salt
> 1 cup whole-wheat flour
> 3-1/2 cups white flour
> 2 tablespoons butter or margarine, melted
> 1/2 cup light brown sugar, packed
> 1 tablespoon ground cinnamon
> 1 cup chopped walnuts
> 1/2 cup raisins soaked in water, drained

Combine water and yeast, stirring until dissolved. Stir in 1 tablespoon sugar. Let stand 15–20 minutes or until yeast begins to bubble. Combine yeast mixture, milk, 1/4 cup melted butter, 2 tablespoons sugar, eggs, and salt in large bowl and mix well. Add whole-wheat flour and mix well. Add enough white flour to make soft dough, stiff enough to knead on floured board until smooth and elastic, adding flour as needed. Place dough in greased bowl and grease top of dough. Cover and let rise until doubled. Pound dough down. Knead briefly and let rest about 10 minutes. Roll out on floured board, drizzle butter over dough. Sprinkle with brown sugar, cinnamon, walnuts, raisins mixture. Roll up jellyroll fashion. Cut roll into 2-inch slices and place into greased pan. Let rise until doubled (30–40 minutes). Bake at 375 degrees 20–25 minutes. Frost with confectioners' frosting. Yields 16 rolls.

Sweet Dough

1 cake yeast
3 teaspoons sugar
1 cup milk, scalded
6 cups flour, sifted
1 can evaporated milk, warmed
1 cup warm water
1 tablespoon butter, melted
2 egg yolks, beaten
1 teaspoon salt

Dissolve yeast and sugar in lukewarm milk. Let rise. Sift flour into bowl. Add warm evaporated milk with 1 cup warm water and melted butter. Add beaten egg yolks, salt, and yeast. Knead well. Cover and set in warm place. Let rise for 2 hours. Roll out dough on floured board. Divide into portions to make rolls or coffee cakes, as desired. Cover and let rest for 15 minutes. Form into desired rolls and place into buttered pans. Allow to rise until doubled in bulk. Brush with melted butter.

Bobalky from Sweet Dough

Roll out on floured breadboard to about one-half inch thickness. Transfer to lightly greased cookie sheet. With edge of teaspoon, pull away, or cut into small pieces, smaller than a walnut. Leave on cookie sheet as you work. Let rise 10 minutes. Bake at 375 degrees 15 minutes or until lightly browned. After cooled, pull *Bobalky* apart, if necessary. Add poppy seed mixture to serve.

Poppy Seed Mixture for *Bobalky*

1-1/2 cups ground poppy seed
1 cup water
3 cups sweet milk, boiled
1 cup sugar

Cook poppy seed with water for 10 minutes. Bring milk and 1 cup sugar to boil. Pour over poppy seed and mix well. Add to *Bobalky* and mix well to serve.

Houska (Christmas Bread) - *Teta* Nettie Bejček-Mráz

5–6 cups unsifted flour, divided
1/2 cup sugar
1-1/2 teaspoons salt
1 teaspoon grated lemon peel
1/4 teaspoon ground mace
2 packages dry yeast
1 cup milk
2/3 cup water
1-1/4 cups butter
2 eggs, room temperature
1/2 cup chopped dark raisins
1/2 cup chopped golden raisins
1 (4-ounce) container mixed citron
1/2 cup almonds, slivered

Cornhusk doll

In a large bowl mix 5-1/2 cups flour, sugar, salt, lemon peel, mace, and undissolved yeast. Combine milk, water, and butter in saucepan. Heat over low heat until hot (120–130 degrees). Butter does not need to melt. Gradually add to dry ingredients and beat 2 minutes at medium speed with electric mixer. Scrape bowl with spatula. Add eggs and 1/2 cup flour. Beat at high speed 2 minutes, scraping bowl with spatula. Turn onto lightly floured board. Knead until smooth and elastic, about 10 minutes. Cover with greased plate and clean towel. Let rest about an hour in warm place. In small bowl, mix raisins, citron, nuts and set aside. Punch down dough. Turn out on lightly floured surface. Knead raisins, citron, and nuts into dough along with flour if needed.

One Large Loaf

Divide dough into 4 equal pieces. Roll 3 pieces into ropes about 15 inches long. Braid the 3 pieces together as you would braid hair. Lay on greased baking sheet. Tuck ends under to seal. Divide remaining piece into three, again, repeat braiding process. Place on top of larger braid. Tuck ends under to seal.

Two Smaller Loaves

Divide dough in half, then each half into thirds. Roll out ropes and braid together. Place in well-greased loaf pan or on cookie sheet. For smaller loaves, omit secondary top braid.

Cover loosely with waxed paper brushed with oil. Top with plastic wrap. Refrigerate 2–24 hours. When ready to bake, remove from refrigerator. Uncover dough carefully. Let stand at room temperature for 10 minutes.

Bake in 350 degree oven for 35–40 minutes. Remove from baking sheet or loaf pans and cool. While warm, may top with confectioners' sugar frosting or leave plain. After a few days, if there is some left, it is very good toasted with butter on it.

Oatmeal Yeast Bread

> 2 cups water
> 1-1/2 cups rolled oats, uncooked
> 1/2 cup molasses
> 1 teaspoon salt
> 2 tablespoons shortening
> 2 packages dry granular yeast
> 1/2 cup lukewarm water
> 6 cups sifted flour (approximately)

Bring water and oatmeal to boil in saucepan. Stir occasionally. Remove from heat immediately when it comes to boil. Stir in molasses, salt, and shortening. Cool to lukewarm. Soften yeast in one half cup lukewarm water in mixing bowl. Stir in lukewarm oatmeal mixture. Add about five cups flour to make stiff dough. Turn onto floured board and knead in remaining cup of flour. Grease a mixing bowl and place dough into it. Turn dough over once so top will be greased. Cover and let rise in warm place until doubled in bulk. Punch dough down with fingertips. Cover and let rise again for about 30 minutes. Toss onto lightly floured board and knead well, adding more flour as needed. Divide dough into 3 loaves and place in three greased standard loaf pans. Cover and let rise in a warm place until doubled in bulk again. Bake in 350 degree oven for about 35 minutes.

Vdolky

Vdolky is a sweet roll that looks like a flat bismarck but doesn't have jelly inside. It is served with prune filling, cottage cheese, and a dollop of sour cream. Very Slovak.

2 packages dry yeast
1/2 cup water, warm
1 cup milk, scalded
3 tablespoons sugar, divided
2 eggs, beaten
5 cups flour
1 stick butter, softened
1 teaspoon salt

Dissolve yeast in warm water, add milk and sugar. After yeast works, add beaten eggs. Mix remaining ingredients as for pie crust. Add yeast mixture. Work together, kneading well. Set aside and allow to rise. When dough is doubled in bulk, roll out to 1/2 inch thickness. You may use a 2-inch biscuit cutter. Place on lightly greased cookie sheets. Set aside and allow to rise again, almost double in bulk. Heat large electric frying pan to 250–300 degrees.

Very lightly grease the bottom of pan, wiping excess off with paper towel. When dough is ready, lay pieces in fry pan, not too close together. They will continue to rise in pan while cooking. Turn over as each piece browns. Do not cover. Brown both sides and edges. This takes time and cannot be rushed. These also may be baked in oven.

Vdolky Topping

1 cup sugar, divided
1 heaping teaspoon cinnamon, divided
1 stick butter, melted
2 cups stewed prunes, pitted and mashed
1 carton small curd cottage cheese (16 ounces)
1 carton sour cream (16 ounces)

Mix together cinnamon and sugar and divide for sprinkling. Dip baked *vdolky* in melted butter. Sprinkle with cinnamon and sugar. Put 2 tablespoons of prune mix on top. Two tablespoons of cottage cheese on top of that. Put large dollop of sour cream on top of that. Sprinkle with additional cinnamon and sugar to serve. You may refrigerate or freeze *vdolky* and heat again for later serving.

Butter Horns

> 2 envelopes granulated yeast
>   (or 2 small cakes compressed yeast)
> 1/2 cup lukewarm water
> 1 tablespoon sugar
> 1 cup milk, scalded
> 1/2 cup sugar
> 1/2 cup shortening
> 3 eggs, beaten
> 2 teaspoons salt
> 6 cups flour, divided
> 1 tablespoon coarse salt
> 1 tablespoon poppy seed
> 1 tablespoon caraway seed

Soften yeast in 1/2 cup lukewarm water. Add 1 tablespoon sugar to yeast mixture. Scald milk and add 1/2 cup sugar, shortening. Stir until shortening is melted. Cool to lukewarm. Stir in eggs, salt, 2 cups flour. Mix on low speed or beat by hand until all is mixed in. Add yeast and beat about 5 minutes. Add 2-3/4 cups flour. Turn out on floured board. Add enough flour (about 1-1/2 cups, but this will vary) to make a soft dough. Knead just enough to shape into a smooth ball. Place in greased bowl, grease top, let rise until double in bulk. Punch down. Let rise again. Punch down and divide dough in half and roll out two 9-inch circles. Cut each circle into 12 wedges. You can make smaller by cutting more than 12, if desired. Brush butter on each wedge and roll up, large end first, to make a crescent. Bend into half-moon shapes, put on lightly greased cookie sheets. You may sprinkle with caraway, poppy seed or coarse salt. Let rise again on sheets. Bake in 375 degree oven for 12 minutes. Check for desired doneness.

Dough for Cottage-Cheese Cake

> 1 cup milk, heated
> 1/4 cup oil
> 1/4 cup sugar
> 1 egg yolk
> 1 package dry yeast
> 2 cups flour
> Dash salt

Add oil and sugar while heating milk. When milk mixture is luke-warm, add 1 egg yolk. Add yeast. Allow to rise for 15 minutes. Add 2 cups flour, and a dash of salt, stirring with wooden spoon. Let rise about 1 hour. Put in greased pie tins. Let dough rise about 15 minutes more. Press down. Fill with cottage cheese filling or any fillings used for *koláčky*. Bake 350 degrees for 25 minutes. Check for doneness.

Sour Cream Crescents

> 2 cups dairy sour cream
> 2 packages dry yeast
> 1/2 cup warm water
> 1/4 cup margarine or butter, softened
> 1/3 cup sugar
> 2 teaspoons salt
> 2 eggs, beaten
> 6 cups flour, divided
> Powdered sugar with nutmeg, optional

Heat sour cream over low heat until chill is taken off. Dissolve yeast in warm water in mixing bowl. Add sour cream, margarine, sugar, salt, eggs, and 2 cups of flour. Beat mixture until lumps are gone. Stir in remaining flour to make a stiff dough. Knead dough on well-floured board until smooth (10 minutes.) Place in greased bowl, turning to bring greased side up. Lightly grease top again. Cover with plastic wrap. Let rise about an hour in warm place until dough doubles. Divide dough into 3 pieces and roll out on floured board. Cut into wedges, 12–14 inches, as if cutting a pie, depending on how large you want them. Spread with any fruit jam or filling. (see page 96). Roll up with wider end first. Put on lightly greased cookie sheet, forming crescent shapes. Bake at 350 degrees for 12 minutes or until golden brown. Remove with spatula and cool. Shake in powdered sugar to serve.

Sour Cream Twists - *Teta* Anna Mráz

> 1 package dry yeast
> 1/4 cup warm water
> 1 egg and 2 yolks, beaten
> 3/4 cup sour cream
> 1 teaspoon vanilla
> 3-1/2 cups flour
> 1 cup butter, softened
> 1 teaspoon salt
>
> Sprinkling mix:
> 1/2 cup sugar, 1 teaspoon cinnamon
> 1/2 teaspoon grated vanilla bean (if available)

Dissolve yeast in water. Add eggs, sour cream, and vanilla. Beat well. Add softened butter and salt and all ingredients to flour. Mix together until smooth. Chill for at least 2 hours, or overnight. Preheat oven to 350 degrees. Divide dough in half. Roll out on sugared surface to a 16 x 8" rectangle. Sprinkle with cinnamon and sugar mixed with vanilla bean. Fold both sides over the long way meeting in the center. Dough will then be doubled with a seam in center. Roll again with rolling pin, to 16 x 8" size; sprinkle again, fold over in like manner, to the center. Roll again, for third time and repeat process, each time sprinkling dough with sugar mixture. Finally, with dough in 16 x 8" rectangle, cut lengthwise into two–16 x 4" strips. Cut thirty-two 4 x 1-inch strips. Twist each one several times and place on ungreased cookie sheet. Press ends down onto sheet as you work. Repeat with second ball of dough. Bake in 350 degree oven for about 15 minutes, being careful not to burn. Makes about 5 dozen twists.

Walnut Roll Dough

1 cup hot milk
1 cup shortening or margarine
2/3 cup sugar
2 teaspoons salt
2 packages granulated yeast
1 cup lukewarm water
3 eggs, beaten
8 cups sifted flour, divided into two parts

Pour hot milk over shortening, sugar, and salt. Dissolve 2 packages granulated yeast in the lukewarm water and add to milk mixture. Add eggs and 4 cups of flour. Mix thoroughly. Add 4 more cups flour a little at a time. Put dough in greased bowl. Cover. Refrigerate overnight. Divide dough into 6 balls. Roll out each one to 9 x 13" shape, using a knife or pizza cutter. Spread filling over dough. Roll in jellyroll fashion, sealing edges with water if necessary. Let rise until double in bulk. Bake at 375 degrees until lightly browned. 15–18 minutes.
Yields 6 rolls.

Walnut Filling

1 pound walnut pieces ground quite fine
1/2 cup sugar
1 teaspoon cinnamon
2 egg whites, beaten
1/4 cup butter or margarine

Mix together first 4 ingredients. Add 1/4 cup melted butter or margarine, and stir with first mixture. Spread over dough. Sprinkle nuts or use poppy seed, prune, apricot, raspberry, or fruit of choice in place of nuts.

Pirohy Dough

It was a "given" with Uncle John's visits, that *pirohy* would be served. The kitchen was bustling, with many hands working. At least once, maybe twice, the phrase, "Many hands make light work" was uttered; in Slovak, of course. Two fillings were used as family favorites.

> 3 eggs
> 1/4 cup water
> 2-1/2 cups flour
>   (perhaps a little more flour
>   enough to make a soft dough)
> 1/2 teaspoon salt
> 1/2 pound butter for serving

While you stir up the dough, the rest of the family should be working on fillings (see page 109). Mix ingredients to form soft dough. Scoop out onto floured bread board and form a large ball. Roll quite thin, into a circle. After making potato and cottage cheese fillings, use palms of your hands to form walnut-sized balls. Place balls side by side in a row at top of circle of dough, working to your right. Fold dough over to cover the balls and allow enough space in between to cut and make small pockets. With sharp knife, cut across bottom of each row and on either side of ball to make pockets. They will look similar to ravioli. Repeat the process until the dough and fillings are used up.

Pinch edges tightly shut on all 3 sides. Set aside on floured towel. Bring two large pots of water to boil. Slide cottage cheese *pirohy* into one pot and potato in the other. Boil gently 12–15 minutes. Remove from heat and remove with soup skimmer or drain in large colander. While *pirohy* are cooking, melt butter in small sauce pan. Put *pirohy* into large bowls and drench with the butter. Sprinkle paprika on top to serve. *Teta* Anna sprinkled nutmeg over the top.

Pirohy Small Batch

> 1 cup flour
> 1 egg
> 4 tablespoons water, approximately

Mix together to form a soft dough (see *pirohy* on previous page for directions). One cup flour makes about 15 large *pirohy*.

Cottage Cheese Filling

> 1/2 pound dry cottage cheese
> 1 egg, beaten
> 1/8 teaspoon salt

If dry cottage cheese is not available, put regular small curd type into piece of cheesecloth or other white clean loose fabric (towel, perhaps). Squeeze out liquid. Mix egg and salt into cottage cheese. Form balls and have ready on large breadboard or clean towel.

Potato Filling

> 2 large potatoes
> 1/2 cup medium Cheddar cheese
>   (more, if desired)
> Small onion, chopped
> 1/4 stick butter

Cook and mash potatoes. Cook onion in butter. Add grated cheese and cooked onion into potatoes and mix well. Cool. Form balls size of a walnut and assemble as directed on page 108. Serve *pirohy* hot with *klobása* or ring baloney.

Slovak *Halušky* One

> 1 pound potatoes
> 2 cups flour
> 1 teaspoon salt
> 1-1/2 teaspoons baking powder
> 1 egg
> 1/2 cup butter
> 1 cup cottage cheese
> 1/2 teaspoon caraway seed

Grind raw potatoes. Mix with flour, salt, baking powder, and egg to make dough. Fill kettle 1/2 full of water. Bring to boil. Roll dough on floured board to 1/2-inch thickness. Cut into 1/2-inch strips, about 2 inches long. Drop into boiling water and return to boil about 4 minutes. Take out with slotted spoon, draining water from each spoon. Brown butter in skillet and add drained *halušky*. Brown and sprinkle with caraway seed. At last minute add cottage cheese and mix just enough to heat.

Halušky Two

> 2 large potatoes
> 1 egg
> 1 teaspoon salt
> 2 cups flour

Peel potatoes and grate them. Add egg, salt, and flour. Stir together with wooden spoon. Add water if dough is too stiff. Drop by teaspoonfuls into boiling water. Cook about 10 minutes. Drain in colander. Rinse and add to fried cabbage (see page 132).

Dumplings with Bacon

> 1/4 pound bacon, fried
> 4 good-sized potatoes
> 2 cups flour
> 1/2 pound feta cheese
> 1/2 teaspoon salt
> 1 tablespoon butter

Fry small pieces of bacon until crisp; drain, and set aside. Peel and grate potatoes. Mix with flour. Add a little water if too stiff. Season. Put on dinner plate for easier handling. Slide spoonfuls from plate into boiling water. Boil for 10 minutes. Drain in colander and rinse. Brown in butter in fry pan. Add bacon and feta cheese. Mix well and serve.

Raised Bread Dumplings

2 slices white bread, cubed
2 tablespoons sweet cream butter
1/2 envelope dry yeast
3/4 cup milk, lukewarm
1 egg
2 cups flour
1 teaspoon salt

Brown bread cubes in butter. Set aside to cool. Sprinkle yeast into lukewarm milk, let rise. Beat egg, add yeast mixture, flour, and salt. Beat thoroughly with wooden spoon. Add bread cubes. Knead and let rise until double in bulk in bowl. Shape dumplings size of small ball. Let rise again on floured board. Cover with clean dish towel.

Bring salted water to full boil. Lower in dumplings gently with slotted spoon. Keep pot covered for 5 minutes. Turn dumplings and boil gently another 5–7 minutes. When done, remove from water with slotted spoon, one at a time. Use 2 forks to open dumpling in half or cut with string.

Škubánky

A little dumpling, sometimes served with sugar and poppy seed, or cabbage.

6 medium-sized potatoes
1 cup water
1-1/2 cups flour, sifted
1 teaspoon salt
1/2 stick butter
3/4 cup raw poppy seed
   with 2 teaspoons sugar

Peel and cook potatoes until done. Drain, reserve liquid, mash potatoes, add 1 cup potato water, more or less, depending on consistency. Add flour and salt and beat again until well mixed. Heat butter in pan and drop potato mixture by spoonfuls into hot frying pan. Brown on both sides. Sprinkle with poppy seed mixture. *Škubánky* may also be made with raw, grated potatoes using the same recipe. Some people add a few grated carrots to this recipe, either cooked or raw.

Mom's Favorite Plum Dumpling Recipe

10–12 pitted Italian plums
Sugar lumps, as many as plums
2-1/2 cups flour
1 tablespoon shortening
1 teaspoon salt
2 teaspoons baking powder
2 eggs, beaten
1/2 cup milk
2 quarts boiling water
Drawn butter
2 cups cottage cheese, heaping
Cinnamon
Sugar

Wash and cut plum almost in half to remove pits. Put sugar lump in center of plum and close. Combine flour, shortening, salt, baking powder, eggs, water. Add water if too stiff. Add flour if too sticky. Cover and let rest for 20 minutes or so. Turn dough out onto floured bread board and roll out. Cut rounds with a large glass or wide mouthed fruit jar. Place plum in center of each piece of dough and pull around plum to seal. Work in palms of hands to make smooth, closed ball. Place in salted boiling water.

Cover and boil gently for 10 minutes. Watch so it doesn't boil over. Remove from water with slotted spoon. Use two forks to break open top of dumpling. Pour drawn butter over each dumpling. Spoon generous amount of cottage cheese over top. Sprinkle with cinnamon and sugar. Serve on platter with large serving spoon.

Peach Dumplings

> 4 large peaches
> Cinnamon
> Sugar
> 1 cup mashed potatoes
> 1 egg, beaten
> 1/4 cup milk (to start)
> 1 heaping cup flour
> 1/2 teaspoon salt

Wash peaches well, remove skins, and cut into chunks. Sprinkle with cinnamon and sugar. Mix potatoes and egg, milk, flour, and salt to make dough. Roll dough out on floured board and cut into squares. Seal a good portion of peach in each square. Drop into boiling salted water. Cook for 15 minutes with lid on. Drain. Sprinkle topping over dumpling to serve.

Topping

> 2/3 cup melted butter
> 3 tablespoons white sugar
> 2 tablespoons bread crumbs
> 3 tablespoons brown sugar

Mix well.

Raw Potato Dumplings

> 3 cups grated raw potatoes
> 3 cups white flour
> 1 egg, beaten
> 1 teaspoon salt

Mother called these "sinkers." Grate potatoes. Drain. Add flour, egg, and salt. If sticky, add more flour. Drop dumplings into boiling water by large spoonfuls or form large balls. Cover, and cook 15–20 minutes. Drain. **Tip:** These are good the next day cut up, browned with onions and butter.

Cooked Potato Dumplings

3 cups potatoes, cooked and mashed
2 eggs, beaten
1 tablespoon salt
2 cups white flour
Melted butter (optional)
Paprika (optional)

Add eggs, salt, and flour to potatoes. Mix well. Turn out and knead on floured board. Shape into 3-inch balls. Lower dumplings into boiling water, lifting from bottom if they settle. When boiling begins again, set timer for 12 minutes. Remove from heat and remove one dumpling. Cut in half to check doneness. If done, remove all to platter. Cut in half to serve. May pour melted butter over top and sprinkle with paprika, if desired.

Potato Dumplings

(small batch)

1 cup potatoes, mashed
1/4 cup milk
1/4 cup farina
2 eggs, beaten
1 teaspoon salt
2 cups flour
Water to boil

Potatoes may be left over or freshly boiled. Mash, with a little milk. Add all other ingredients except water. Mix well and turn out on floured board. Roll with hands into a log, patting firmly. Cut 2-inch pieces, larger if you want bigger dumplings.

Immerse in boiling water. Put lid on, but when boiling hard, turn heat down. Cook 15 to 20 minutes, drain and serve.

Riced Potato Dumplings

4 cups riced potatoes
1/2 cup farina
1 egg
1 teaspoon salt
1–3/4 cups flour
2 quarts water

Process cooked potatoes through a potato ricer. Add farina and mix. Should yield 4 cups. Add the egg. Mix. Add salt to flour and gradually add to potato mixture. Mix well. Form dumplings into balls with your hands and lay on floured board, rest for 15–20 minutes. Bring pot of water to boil. Add dumplings and boil for 15 minutes without removing lid. Drain, cut with string (see page 163 for instructions) and serve on platter.

Homemade Noodles

3 eggs
1 cup half-and-half (half cream, half milk)
1/2 teaspoon salt
1/2 teaspoon baking powder
2-1/2 to 3 cups flour

Mix ingredients thoroughly and turn onto floured breadboard. Roll out very thin with rolling pin that has been floured. Don't be afraid to use the flour. Cut in desired width strips or squares. Let dry in open air for 2–3 hours. The noodles can be stored or used right away in soups or a casserole. One-inch square noodles are used for ham and noodle dish.

*Design on a Slovak
tablecloth*

Pancakes

Cooked Potato Pancakes

> 2 cups mashed potatoes
> 2 eggs
> 3 cups flour, divided
> 1/4 teaspoon salt

Mix altogether with 2-1/2 cups flour to make soft dough. Take dough size of golf ball, roll out flat and thin to a six-to-eight inch circle on floured board using remaining flour. Grease griddle and brown pancake on both sides. Spread with butter and raspberry jelly, roll up jellyroll style. Dust with powdered sugar. Mother made these for us in the morning before we went to school.

Mother's note: Serve with butter and jelly, or, if you're Norwegian, leave the eggs out, eat these cold, as bread, and call it *lefse*.

Raw Potato Pancakes

> 6 potatoes, grated
> 2 eggs
> 1/2 onion, grated
> 2 tablespoons flour
> Pinch salt
> 1/4 cup milk

Grate potatoes and drain off liquid. Add eggs, onion, flour, salt, and milk. Drop by spoonfuls onto hot griddle using goose grease or lard to fry. Serve with granulated sugar sprinkled over the top.

Slovak Maxims: Mother was a great one for maxims. They were part of our education. Here are some she frequently used that became engrained in us.

> *What's cooked at home should be eaten at home.*
> *Čo varíš doma, má ostať doma.*

> *There are things you can only see with eyes that have cried.*
> *Sú veci, ktoré možno vidieť len očami, ktoré plakali.*

Palacinky

Palacinky is a pancake, like a crepe, but I have never heard it referred to as anything but *palacinky*.

>   3/4 cup skim milk
>   3/4 cup cold water
>   2 egg whites
>   1-1/2 cups sifted flour
>   1/3 cup margarine, melted
>   2 tablespoons rum or orange liqueur
>   1 tablespoon sugar
>   4 drops yellow food coloring

Blend all ingredients together and pour 1/4 cup batter into hot oiled skillet. Turn skillet to cover bottom completely. Flip with pancake turner, browning both sides. Serve with butter and jelly or syrup. Roll up to eat.

Cornhusk doll with churn

Cornhusk doll with baby

Meat, Fish, & Poultry

Many of the following recipes came from *Teta* Anna Mráz. *Teta* Anna left home and worked as a domestic before she was fifteen years of age. In her early twenties, after moving to Pittsburgh, the Supervisor of the cafeteria at the University of Pittsburgh hired her and reportedly taught her everything she knew about cooking for large groups and restaurant management. Later, when *Teta* Anna moved to Chicago, she got a job at Cuneo Press cafeteria and before long was promoted to manager. She remained at that job until she and Uncle Victor bought a business in Phillips and returned home.

Stuffed Beef Rolls

> 2 pounds round steak, 1/2 inch thick
> 1 cup flour
> Desired seasonings (garlic salt, salt, pepper)
> Prepared mustard
> 4 strips bacon, fried limp, not crisp
> 1 small onion, minced
> 2 teaspoons dried parsley
> 4 dill pickles cut into halves
> 1/4 cup oil
> 2 tablespoons tomato paste
> 2-1/2 cups water
> 2 beef bouillon cubes
> 2 teaspoons caraway seed

Preheat oven to 300 degrees. Pound beef with wooden tenderizer until 1/4 inch thick. Cut into 8 pieces. Roll in flour mixed with desired seasonings. Spread mustard on each piece, with 1 strip bacon in center of each piece. Sprinkle with onion and parsley. Place piece of pickle on end closest to you. Roll up jellyroll fashion, and tie with string. Heat the oil. Cook rolls over medium heat in frying pan until brown on all sides. Remove to roaster and put in oven. To frying pan, add water, bouillon, and flour to make a smooth paste. Stir in tomato paste and caraway seed. Heat to boiling then reduce heat. Pour over beef rolls and bake in oven for 1-1/2 hours. Remove strings by snipping with kitchen shears.

Hungarian Goulash

Dr. Frederike Kastenbauer (Dad's cousin), Vienna, Austria

> 2 pounds round steak, 1-1/2 inch thick
> 6 tablespoons flour
> 1/2 cup butter or oil
> 1 large onion, minced
> 2 teaspoons paprika
> 1 teaspoon salt
> 1/2 teaspoon pepper
> 1 clove garlic, minced
> 2 teaspoons marjoram
> 1 teaspoon caraway seed
> 1 teaspoon cider vinegar
> 1/2 cup water

Cut steak into 2-inch cubes. Roll in flour. In skillet, melt butter or oil, sauté onion until limp. Add steak and brown meat on all sides. Add paprika, salt, pepper, garlic, marjoram, caraway seed, and cider vinegar. Add water. Cover and simmer slowly until meat is tender, 1-1/2 to 2 hours.

Remove cover, continue to simmer until goulash is thickened. Serve over hot, wide noodles.

Pickled Beef or Venison

> 3 pounds beef or venison, cut into small chunks

Brine

> 1 cup vinegar
> 1 cup water
> 2 tablespoons pickling spice (*in bag)
> 1 small onion, minced
> 1 teaspoon salt

* Make bag from 4 x 4" piece of cheese cloth or loose knit fabric. Place spices in center, gather up and tie top together with string. Trim excess material from top.

Mix all brine ingredients together. Soak meat in brine for 24 hours (or more if desired) in refrigerator. Remove spice bag and simmer meat in brine until tender, adding water as needed.

Gravy

1/2 pint heavy cream
Flour and water to thicken
1 tablespoon sugar

Remove meat, add cream, flour, and water to thicken as for gravy, and heat. Before serving, burn 1 tablespoon of sugar over medium heat, and add to gravy. May add more sugar if sweeter gravy is desired. Serve over mashed potatoes or potato dumplings.

Liver

6 slices calf liver, 1/4 inch thick
12 bacon slices
1/4 cup flour
1/4 teaspoon garlic salt
1/4 teaspoon celery salt
1/4 teaspoon paprika
1 large onion, sliced
3/4 cup wine or homemade beer

Set oven at 300 degrees. In large skillet, sauté bacon until crisp. Remove and pat off excess grease with paper towel. Put into pan inside oven to keep warm. Mix flour and seasonings together and coat liver on both sides. Heat bacon grease to very hot.

Sauté liver quickly, turning once. A few minutes on each side is enough, or until blood cooks out. Don't overcook. Remove meat from pan and add to bacon in oven. Pour off excess grease in pan, leaving a little, then sauté onions until soft. Using same skillet, add wine or beer. Heat to boiling stage. Remove bacon and liver from oven. Arrange liver on platter with bacon served on side. Pour onions and wine/beer over liver.

Note: Parsley buttered potatoes and fresh string beans go well with this dish, along with cabbage slaw.

Veal Paprika

> 2 pounds veal cut into chunks
> 1/2 cup flour
> 1/4 teaspoon garlic salt
> 2 teaspoons paprika
> Salt and pepper
> 4 slices bacon, fried
> Bacon drippings for browning meat
> 1 cup water
> 1 small carton sour cream (16 ounces)

Dredge meat in flour mixed with seasonings. Fry bacon and remove from pan. Brown meat in drippings. Add water to meat and bring to boil. Cook on low heat for 1-1/2 hours until tender, adding water as needed. Crumble bacon. When meat is done, turn off heat, but keep warm. Stir in sour cream, bacon, and more paprika.

Serve over raised bread dumplings, *halušky*, or homemade noodles (see pages 109, 111, 115).

Pickled beets and lime gelatin salad go well with this dish.

Baked Beef or Veal Tongue

> 4–5 pound beef or veal tongue
> Celery leaf tops, chopped
> 1 large onion, cut into chunks
> 2 large bay leaves
> 1 garlic clove, minced fine
> 1 teaspoon pickling spice
> 1 tablespoon salt

Wash tongue thoroughly under running water. Scrape membranes from it. Put tongue into large kettle. Add enough water to cover. Add celery leaves, onion, bay leaf, garlic, pickling spice, and salt. Boil gently for 1-1/2 to 2 hours, depending on tenderness. While cooking tongue, prepare the following ingredients:

1 cup cooking broth
1 tablespoon cornstarch
4 carrots, coursely ground
1 cup diced celery
1 onion diced
1/2 green pepper, diced
2 cups tomatoes, chopped
Pepper and salt to taste

Remove tongue from broth and peel while it is still warm. Slice. Put meat in roaster, mix broth with cornstarch and add the vegetables to roaster. Cover and bake 1 hour at 350 degrees. Bake additional 15 minutes with cover off. Stir. Good with mashed or boiled potatoes.

Scrambled Eggs and Calf Brains - Vicki Voda Weber

2 quarts boiling water
1 teaspoon salt
1 teaspoon lemon juice
1/2 pound calf brains
2 tablespoons butter
1 medium-sized onion, chopped
6 eggs, beaten
1 teaspoon salt
Pepper to taste
Cream as needed
Fresh chives or parsley

Bring pot of salted water to boil. Add lemon juice. Add brains and poach until tender. Remove, strain, and keep warm in oven. Melt butter over medium heat. Sauté onion. Pour eggs into fry pan with butter and onions, add salt and pepper. Scramble eggs and add brains when eggs are almost done. Make sure they don't dry out. A little cream may be added, when done. Mix brains and eggs and serve on platter with toast or biscuits. Garnish with fresh chives or parsley.

Pork or Ham with Noodles

> 2 large eggs
> 1 cup milk
> 4 cups of cooked homemade noodles
>   cut into small squares
> 2 cups ham, diced
> Salt and pepper
> 1/2 stick of butter

Beat eggs and milk. Butter a deep ovenproof bowl. Layer noodles and ham while adding a little milk mixture, salt, pepper, and a little butter over each layer. Repeat until everything is used. Cover and bake 45 minutes in 350 degree oven. Stir a few times early in baking. Uncover and bake another 15–20 minutes until top is brown and edges are crisp.

Chicken Paprika

> 1 chicken, washed and cut up
> Water, enough to cover
> 1/2 small can cooked tomatoes, chopped fine
> 2 teaspoons paprika
> 1/2 cup diced celery
> 1/4 cup diced onion
> 1/4 teaspoon of celery salt
> 1 carton sour cream (16 ounces) or
>   1 pint of half-and-half
> 2 tablespoons flour

Place chicken in pot with water and cook for 1/2 hour with lid on. Add all ingredients except sour cream. Cook for additional 1/2 hour or until chicken is tender. Remove chicken from broth, put into serving bowl. Thicken gravy with one pint of sour cream mixed with the flour. Add more paprika, if desired.

Sometimes mother made this with half-and-half (1/2 cream and 1/2 milk). Use 1 pint with flour enough to make a gravy, as for white sauce. Stir into simmering broth. Serve over bread dumplings or small soup dumplings. Both are good!

Roast Goose with Pork Sausage Dressing

1 goose, 4–5 pounds

Wash goose well, inside and out. Rub inside of bird with garlic salt. Stuff with pork sausage dressing (see below). Stuff bird and roast at 450 degrees for 30–45 minutes. Leave uncovered until it begins to brown, reduce heat to 350 degrees and continue roasting, covered, until fork tender, about 2 hours. Take cover off for the last 1/2 hour. Allow enough time in case goose is tough and needs to roast longer!

Pork Sausage Dressing

> 4 pork sausage links (or 1/2 roll of pork sausage meat)
> 2 cups bread crumbs
> 2 eggs
> Salt and pepper
> Small onion, minced
> 1 teaspoon sage
> 1 teaspoon marjoram
> 1 stalk celery, cut fine
> 1/2 cup milk

If using sausage links, squeeze meat out into the bowl. Mix all ingredients together and blend well. Stuff bird and sew cavity shut with needle and string.

Muskie Boil

> 1 muskie
> Water enough to cover
> 3 bay leaves
> 1/2 teaspoon garlic salt
> 1 tablespoon pickling spice (put into small cloth bag, tie with store string)
> 1/2 teaspoon caraway seed

Clean and skin fish. Cut fish into 3-inch chunks, cutting through bone. Bring water to boil with all ingredients and immerse fish. Boil for at least 10 minutes depending on size. Don't overcook.

Fish is done when firm and white. Remove from water, drain and serve with drawn butter. Serve with parsley buttered potatoes and vegetables. Muskie is bony, so be careful!

Broiled Trout

>5–6 brook trout
>
>Marinade:
>1/4 cup salad oil or olive oil
>1/4 cup soy sauce
>2 tablespoons fresh lemon juice
>2 tablespoons sugar

Wash fish thoroughly. Trout do not need to be scaled, but slit belly open and clean out innards. May leave heads on, if desired. Mix together all ingredients for marinade and marinate fish 1 hour or so. Broil on each side for 7 to 10 minutes. Baste generously every few minutes with marinade. Remove from oven and serve.

Walleye

>6 pieces of walleye fillets cut into 2–3 inch chunks
>2 eggs, beaten
>1/2 cup milk
>1 cup flour
>1/2 teaspoon garlic salt
>1/2 teaspoon celery salt
>1/2 teaspoon paprika
>2 cups coarsely ground soda cracker crumbs
>1/2 cup cooking oil, more if needed

Preheat oven to 300 degrees. Beat egg and milk together in bowl. Dredge walleye in flour mixed with the seasonings. Dip into egg/milk mixture, roll in cracker crumbs. Fry in hot oil. Remove and put into pan in oven until ready to serve.

Beer Batter Fish

1 pound cleaned smelt (other fish may be used)
1 cup all-purpose flour and 1/2 cup, separated
1 teaspoon baking powder
1/2 teaspoon salt
1 egg, lightly beaten
2 tablespoons vegetable oil
2/3 cup milk
1/3 cup beer
Vegetable oil for frying
Lemon wedges, optional
1 jar tartar sauce, optional
Parsley for garnish

In large bowl sift together 1 cup flour, baking powder, and salt. In another bowl beat egg, oil, and milk. Gradually stir milk mixture and beer into the flour mixture, beating with fork until lumps are gone. Heat enough oil in saucepan to measure about 2 inches. Dip fish into flour, then batter to coat. Fry a few pieces at a time for 5–7 minutes until crisp and brown. Drain on paper towels. Serve with lemon wedges or tartar sauce. Garnish with parsley.

Baked Carp

3 pounds carp
1 tablespoon lemon juice
Seasoned salt
Mashed garlic
1/2 cup butter, melted
1/2 teaspoon caraway seed

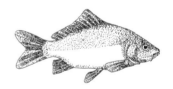

Cut fish in half lengthwise after cleaning thoroughly. Lay in shallow pan and sprinkle with lemon juice and seasonings. Drizzle butter and caraway seed over top of fish and bake in 350 degree oven for 30–45 minutes. Check on doneness. Serve with drawn butter.

Pan Fish Fry

Fresh pan fish
1 cup buttermilk pancake flour
1/2 teaspoon seasoned salt (or more to taste)
1 egg, beaten
1/2 cup milk
1 cup bread crumbs
1/2 cup oil for frying, more if needed

Remove heads, scales, and innards. Rinse fish thoroughly. Pat dry with absorbent towel. Put flour and seasonings in bag and shake fish in it. Dip in combined egg and milk mixture. Roll in bread crumbs on flat plate. Fry in heated oil until brown and crisp on both sides. Keep in heated oven until ready to serve.

Fish Patties - Annie Peroutka

10 small fish, filleted or
  a muskie cut into chunks, raw
10–12 soda crackers, crushed
1 cup milk
2 eggs, beaten
1 tablespoon lemon juice
1/2 teaspoon salt
1/2 teaspoon pepper
1 tablespoon chopped parsley
1/4 cup chopped onion
1/4 cup chopped green pepper (optional)
Oil or butter for frying
Tartar sauce

Fillet fish and cut into pieces. Grind in meat grinder or food processor. Soak soda cracker crumbs in 1 cup milk and add beaten eggs and lemon juice. Mix into the ground fish. Season with salt and pepper. Add parsley, chopped onion, and green pepper. Shape in hands, like round pancake, and flatten with spatula in fry pan. Fry in oil or butter until golden. Serve with tartar sauce.

Pickled Fish

Muskie, northern, or other large fish, cut into chunks
1 cup white sugar
1 tablespoon pickling spice
2 cups white vinegar
1 cup white port wine
1 medium onion, sliced

May adjust amounts of ingredients in proportion to the amount of fish used. Debone as much as possible. Cut into chunks and soak in salt water brine (water with salt added; strong enough to float an egg). Refrigerate 24 hours. Boil sugar, spice, vinegar, and wine together in saucepan, stirring until sugar is dissolved. Cool. Drain fish from salt-water brine. Cover with second brine, add sliced onions, and refrigerate for several days. Bones become soft during this process. May add sour cream and chives to drained pickled fish for variety.

Vegetables

Mother believed in pushing the vegetables and was very creative in doing so. She had many ways of slipping them to us!

Dried Peas and Sauerkraut

A meal almost forgotten until I began searching memory for meals passed on from Grandma Mráz and made by my mother.

1 pound whole dried peas (yellow or green)
8 cups water
1 medium onion, chopped fine
2 tablespoons butter

Wash whole yellow or green peas, sort, and soak overnight. Drain. Cover with water and cook in small kettle for a very long time (2–3 hours) or until peas are done. Brown onion in small skillet with butter. Add to peas, mixing thoroughly. Season to taste. Serve with cold raw sauerkraut and hot slices of ham. This was a favorite Sunday dinner.

Spiced Tomato Gravy

1 pint tomatoes
1 pint water
1 small onion, chopped
1 teaspoon pickling spice
2 tablespoons flour for thickening
1/2 cup water
Salt
2 tablespoons sugar
2 tablespoons cider vinegar

Cook tomatoes in water with small onion and pickling spice for about one hour on low heat. When simmered down, take from heat and strain through sieve or strainer. Put liquid back into kettle. Make flour thickening for gravy. Thicken to desired consistency. May need to add water. Add salt, sugar, and vinegar. Stir well and heat to boiling. Take from heat. Taste and adjust vinegar or sugar, accordingly. Salt to taste. Serve over bread dumplings. This was served with soup meat, after liver dumpling soup.

Dill Gravy

1/2 cup tender sprigs of dill (dill weed)
2 cups water
1 pint half-and-half (half cream, half milk)
1 egg
1/4 cup cider vinegar
Salt and pepper to taste

Rinse dill and put into kettle with 2 cups water, and simmer for 20 minutes. Add 1 pint half-and-half, heat to boiling, but don't boil. Remove from heat. Add 1 egg and stir with fork. Add vinegar, salt, and pepper to taste. Serve over boiled potatoes.

Slovak dolls and other artifacts shown are from the collection of Toni Brendel.

Garden Carrots

4 good-sized carrots, sliced
1 large onion, sliced
1/4 stick butter
1/2 cup snipped, fresh parsley
1/8 teaspoon salt, or to taste
1/8 teaspoon pepper, or to taste

Slice carrots into 1/8 inch slices. Cook partially. Don't overcook. Sauté onion in butter. Add carrots and sauté together before serving. Add generous amount of snipped parsley. Add additional butter if desired. Salt and pepper to taste.

Escalloped Potatoes

6 good-sized potatoes
1/2 stick of butter or oleo
1 cup milk, divided
2 tablespoons flour
Salt and pepper

Butter a casserole dish. Peel and slice potatoes. Make a white sauce: melt butter or oleo in sauce pan. Pour 1/4 cup milk into small jar, add flour, and shake well. Heat remaining milk on low and increase heat while stirring in thickener. Continue stirring until thickened, then mix with sliced potatoes. Season with salt and pepper and bake in 350 degree oven for 1-1/2 hours, increasing heat if desired.

Sweet-Sour Red Cabbage

    1 large head red cabbage, chopped
    1 teaspoon salt
    1/2 cup vinegar
    1/2 cup water
    1/2 cup granulated sugar
    1/4 teaspoon pepper
    1/4 cup bacon grease for frying
    1/2 teaspoon caraway seed

In large bowl, toss cabbage with salt. Let stand about an hour, stirring occasionally. In saucepan, combine vinegar, water, sugar, and pepper. Simmer until sugar is dissolved. In large frying pan, fry cabbage in bacon grease until desired consistency. Add caraway seed. Pour liquid over cabbage and continue to simmer until time to serve. May be served alone or with a favorite dumpling recipe!

Creamed Cabbage

    1 head cabbage, chopped
    1 small onion, chopped
    1/4 cup butter
    1 cup milk
    1/4 cup flour, scant
    1 tablespoon butter, melted
    Salt and pepper
    Paprika

Cook cabbage and onion together in the butter. When almost done, add milk thickened with flour and add 1 tablespoon melted butter. Stir. Add seasonings to serve. Paprika makes it more attractive.

Slovak Sauerkraut

    1 large onion, chopped
    1/2 stick butter or margarine, divided (half to
      brown onion; half to brown flour)
    1 quart sauerkraut
    1/2 teaspoon caraway seed, if desired

2 tablespoons flour
1/8 teaspoon salt
1/8 teaspoon pepper
1/2 cup water
2 tablespoons brown sugar

Brown large onion in butter or margarine. Remove onion and set frying pan aside. Rinse sauerkraut and put into large kettle with 1 cup water. Add onion and caraway seed to sauerkraut and simmer for 1/2 hour. Use frying pan to brown flour (*zápražka*) in remaining butter with salt and pepper. When very dark, add water and make a thin paste. Simmer. Add to sauerkraut. Add 2 tablespoons brown sugar and stir. Simmer for another 1/2 hour on low.

Fried Cabbage with *Halušky*

1 head cabbage, chopped fine
1 small onion, chopped fine
1/4 cup butter or bacon drippings
Salt
Pepper
Paprika

Brown onion in butter. Add cabbage with seasonings. Fry slowly, covered, until brown, 20 to 30 minutes. Add *halušky* (see pages 109–110) and brown a bit before serving, or serve plain.

Corn Pudding

1/2 cup milk
1 egg, beaten
2 tablespoons flour
1 pint cream-style corn
1 pint whole kernel corn
Salt and pepper

Mix milk with egg and add flour. Beat until lumps disappear. Add corn and stir. Season. Grease small casserole bowl. Turn ingredients into it. Bake in 375 degree oven for 45 minutes or until firm.

Sweet-Sour String Beans

> 1/2 cup white granulated sugar
> 1/2 cup cider vinegar
> 1/2 cup water
> 2 pints cut string beans, drained
> 5 slices bacon, fried crisp and crumbled

Heat and stir sugar in vinegar and water until dissolved. Heat beans and pour liquid over them. Add crumbled bacon. Mix to serve.

Wild Mushrooms and Eggs

Although there are many varieties of wild mushrooms, the most commonly found in the northwoods of Wisconsin and wooded areas of eastern Iowa are morels in the spring and button mushrooms in the fall. Wet springs and falls are the best guarantees of an ample harvest.

Mushrooms may be dried and used at a later date. The old method of doing so was to use a needle and thread, pierce the mushroom, and hang it to dry in a heated place.

Mushroom hunting is a part of the lore of Slovakia, the country left behind by our ancestors. The Czech Village in Cedar Rapids, Iowa features *Houby* (mushroom) Days, with an award to the finder of the largest mushroom.

> 4 cups mushrooms
> 1 medium-sized onion, diced
> 6–8 eggs
> Salt and pepper
> Caraway seed

Wash and cut up fresh mushrooms. Sauté onion in butter and add mushrooms. Simmer about 10 minutes. Beat eggs and add to mushrooms and onion. Sprinkle in caraway seeds. Continue to stir with wooden spoon until eggs are cooked as desired.

Pickles

Crock Pickles or "Half-Dones"
Teta Nettie Bejček Mráz

> 1 gallon water
> 1 teacup of pickling salt
> Pinch of alum
> 15 medium-sized cucumbers, 4–5 inches in length
> 4 dill stalks

Bring to boil, water, pickling salt, and alum. Line small crock with 2 stalks of dill, washed and folded to fit. Lay washed cucumbers on top of dill, and cover with remaining dill. Pour hot, hot brine over cucumbers. Be sure to cover completely. Press pickles down and cover with plate weighted with heavy object. Let stand at least a week. Do not refrigerate.

Watermelon Pickles

> Watermelon (see directions below)
> Green leaves of watermelon or grapevine (if available)
> Sugar (as directed)
> 1 teaspoon pulverized alum
> 1 pint of water (as directed)
> 1 beaten egg white (as directed)
> Lemon (as directed)

Remove the melon flesh and skin and cut rind into small-sized pieces. Weigh the pieces and allow to each pound of watermelon, one-and-a-half pounds of sugar. Line a large kettle with the green vine leaves, lay in the melon rind, a layer of vine leaves, and layer of rind. Cover with water and add a teaspoonful of pulverized alum. Cover with a thick cloth and simmer for two hours. Drain. Spread the rind on dishes to cool.

   Dissolve sugar, using a pint of water for every pound and a half of sugar and mix with the beaten white of an egg. Boil and skim the sugar mixture. When clear add the rind and cook two hours.

Take out rind, boil the syrup again, pour over the rind, and let remain standing all night at room temperature.

Next morning remove rind, boil the syrup, and add lemon juice using one lemon to a quart of syrup. When it is thick enough to drop from a spoon in heavy drops, it is done. Put rind into sterilized jars and cover with the syrup. Follow instructions for sealing. Citron melons may be preserved in the same way.

Bread and Butter Pickles

4 quarts sliced cucumbers, unpeeled
6 medium-sized onions, sliced
6 garlic cloves, sliced
1 green pepper, sliced
1 sweet red pepper (or pimiento) sliced
1/3 cup salt

Mix ingredients together. Let stand for 3 hours with cracked ice to cover. Drain well.

Combine in saucepan:
3 cups white vinegar
5 cups sugar
1-1/2 teaspoons turmeric
1-1/2 teaspoons celery seed
2 teaspoons mustard seed
1/4 teaspoon alum

Bring all ingredients to boil, stir to dissolve sugar, then cool. Put drained cucumbers into large kettle. Pour hot brine liquid ingredients over the top. Bring to a boil and remove from heat. Put into sterile pint jars. Wipe tops and sides of jars to clean off juice. Seal as directed. Makes 8 pints of pickles.

Raw Pickle Chips

 4 cups vinegar
 4 cups granulated sugar
 1/2 cup salt
 2 cups water
 2 stalks dill
 6 small onions, sliced
 1 gallon raw sliced cucumbers, unpeeled
 1 large green pepper, sliced
 1 gallon jar, sterilized
 1 quart jar, sterilized

Boil vinegar, sugar, salt, and water for 5 minutes to dissolve sugar. Stir. Put dill into bottom of gallon jar and some in bottom of quart jar. Place raw onion, cucumbers, green pepper in alternating layers. About midway, use another dill stalk, layering onion, etc. on top of it. Pour hot vinegar brine over all. Seal in jars and refrigerate. May use as a relish or salad as needed. Keeps indefinitely in refrigerator.

Pickled Vegetables

 1 cup cauliflower florets
 2 cups broccoli tops and stems
   sliced into bite-sized pieces
 2 cups whole small mushrooms
 1 green pepper, bite-sized chunks
 1 large carrot cut into 1/2-inch slices

Marinade

 2 teaspoons pickling spice
   (wrapped in cheesecloth, tied with string)
 1 cup white vinegar
 1/2 cup salad oil
 1/2 cup sugar
 1 clove garlic, peeled
 1 small onion, sliced thin
 4 grinds of pepper from pepper mill

Steam vegetables until crisp-tender, beginning with longer to cook: carrots, cauliflower, broccoli. Allow only 2 minutes for mushrooms, green pepper. Don't overcook. Combine marinade ingredients in large saucepan, bringing to boil. Cool and remove spice bag. Pour marinade over vegetables. Cover and refrigerate for at least 24 hours before serving. May be kept in refrigerator for about 1 month.

Pickled Beets

1-1/2 cups water
1-1/2 cups sugar
3/4 cup cider vinegar
2 three-inch cinnamon sticks
2 pounds cooked and peeled, sliced beets
2 medium-sized onions, sliced

Add water to pan with sugar, vinegar, and cinnamon sticks. Heat to boiling. Keep stirring with wooden spoon until sugar is dissolved. Pour over beets and onions. Cover. Refrigerate overnight.

Pickled Wild Mushrooms

About 2 quarts of fresh mushrooms
1 cup sugar
1-1/8 cups cider vinegar
1 cup water
1 teaspoon caraway seed
Several small onions, sliced

Clean fresh mushrooms carefully. Rinse in colander several times. Boil on low heat about 10 minutes in salted water. Drain and wash again. Set aside and bring sugar, vinegar, and water to a boil. Add caraway seeds and onions. Let simmer a few minutes and add mushrooms. Bring to boil again and just heat mushrooms through.

Put into sterilized pint jars and cool seal. Will yield about 2 pints of pickled mushrooms once they are cooked down. If more, refrigerate and use.

Pickled Bologney

    1 ring of bologney
    2 cups water
    1-1/2 cups cider vinegar
    1 teaspoon salt
    2 tablespoons sugar
    10 peppercorns
    1 teaspoon allspice
    1 large onion, sliced

Cook ring bologney for 1/2 hour. Cool and cut into small slices. Boil together water, vinegar, salt, sugar, peppercorns, and allspice. Simmer until salt and sugar are dissolved. Cool.

Layer bologney and onions in large jar. Pour liquid over the top and refrigerate for at least 24 hours.

Pies and Cakes

Pie Crust

    2 cups flour
    1 teaspoon salt
    3/4 cup lard or shortening
    5 tablespoons cold water

Combine flour and salt in bowl. Cut lard into flour using pastry blender to form pea-size chunks. Sprinkle water one spoon at a time. Toss lightly with fork until dough forms a ball. Divide in half, using half for each crust. Flour board. Roll out into two 9-inch circles. Sprinkle countertop with water. Cover with a piece of waxed paper and roll crust to desired size. Ease into pie plate. Repeat process with second crust. Put desired filling into crust and moisten edge of crust. Cover with second crust. Fold under and flute. Snip top with scissors to allow steam to escape.

Butterscotch Meringue Pie

Baked 9-inch crust
3 egg yolks
1 cup brown sugar
3-1/2 tablespoons cornstarch, mixed with a little water
2 cups milk
1/4 teaspoon salt
3 tablespoons butter
1 teaspoon vanilla

Beat egg yolks and sugar. Mix cornstarch with a little water to make a smooth paste. Add to first mixture, add milk and salt.

Cook in double boiler until thick. Remove from heat, add butter and vanilla. Cool, pour into prepared crust. Make meringue, spread over top of pie and bake at 400 degrees for 10–12 minutes until meringue is golden brown.

Meringue

2 egg whites
1/8 teaspoon salt
1/8 teaspoon cream of tartar
1/2 cup sugar

Beat egg whites until soft peaks form, add salt. Add cream of tartar and sugar. Beat to blend well, but not too dry. Turn out onto pie, sealing edges.

Old-fashioned Pumpkin Pie

2/3 cup brown sugar
2 tablespoons cane sugar
1 teaspoon cinnamon
1/2 teaspoon ginger
1/4 teaspoon cloves
1/4 teaspoon nutmeg
1-3/4 cups pumpkin, cooked, strained
2 large eggs
1/3 teaspoon salt
1-3/4 cups milk
Unbaked pie shell, edges crimped

Preheat oven to 400 degrees. Mix sugars with spices and add to the cooked and strained pumpkin. Add beaten eggs, salt, and milk. Pour into 9-inch unbaked pie crust. Start to bake in hot oven at 400 degrees until edges start to brown. Turn down heat to 350. Pie is done when inserted knife comes out clean. Allow approximately 1-1/2 hours for baking.

Rhubarb Custard Pie

1-1/2 cups sugar
2 unbeaten eggs
1/2 teaspoon salt
2 tablespoons cornstarch, mixed with a little milk
1 cup sour cream
2-1/2 cups diced fresh rhubarb
Double crust for pie

Mix sugar into eggs and beat. Add salt. Mix cornstarch into a small amount of milk and make paste. Add it to sour cream and fold into rhubarb. Mix all together and put into prepared unbaked pie shell. Have top pie crust ready to put over top of pie. Make slits in it to allow steam to escape. Bake in 350–400 degree oven for 1 hour. Check for doneness and if more time is needed, leave in oven another 15 minutes. If edges are getting too dark, cover with aluminum foil.

Rhubarb Pie - Annie Peroutka

3 eggs, beaten
2-1/2 tablespoons milk
2 cups sugar
4 tablespoons flour
3/4 teaspoon nutmeg
4 cups diced rhubarb
2 tablespoons butter, melted
Double crust for pie

Beat eggs and add milk, sugar, and flour. Add nutmeg and rhubarb. Put all in unbaked pie shell. Drizzle butter over top of ingredients in pie shell. Cover with second pie crust and crimp edges to seal. Snip steam holes in top with scissors. Bake at 400 degrees for 50 to 60 minutes. May turn down heat to 350 if browning too fast.

Johnny Cake

Mother would make this in a large black skillet the lumbermen called a "spider." She would serve it to us for breakfast, before school, on cold winter days.

> 1/2 cup white sugar
> 1 teaspoon salt
> 1-1/2 cups cornmeal
> 3/4 cup flour
> 1 heaping teaspoon soda
> 1 egg
> 1-1/2 cups sour milk
> 2 tablespoons lard for greasing pan

Mix dry ingredients together and add liquids to make thick batter. Mix well with wooden spoon. Pour into greased frying pan or baking pan. Bake in 350 oven for 30 minutes. Reduce heat if getting too brown. Serve with butter and honey.

Mincemeat

> 1 pint chopped green tomatoes
> 1-1/2 pints chopped tart apples
> 1 pound raisins, chopped
> 1 cup suet from beef or venison, chopped
> 2 teaspoons each: cinnamon, salt, all-spice, cloves
> 3 cups sugar
> 1/4 cup vinegar
> 1 cup water

Mix all chopped ingredients. Add spices, sugar, vinegar, and water. Put into pot to cook. Simmer until thick. Refrigerate for pie.

Sponge Cake

6 eggs, separated
6 tablespoons cold water
1-1/2 cups sugar
1-1/2 cups cake flour
1/4 teaspoon salt
1 teaspoon baking powder
1 teaspoon vanilla

Beat egg yolks until thick, adding 1 tablespoon cold water for each yolk. Add sugar and beat again. Sift flour, salt, and baking powder three or four times. Add to egg yolks and sugar. Beat egg whites and fold into batter last, a little at a time to completely blend mixture. Add flavoring. Mix well and put into greased 9x13" cake pan.

Bake at 325 degrees for 1 hour or until an inserted toothpick comes out clean. Serve with whipped cream on top. This is good as strawberry shortcake.

Old-fashioned Spice Cake

1 cup white sugar
1/2 teaspoon nutmeg
1 teaspoon cinnamon
1/4 teaspoon allspice
1/2 cup shortening
1/2 cup dark Karo® syrup
1 teaspoon baking soda
1 cup buttermilk
3 whole eggs, beaten
2 cups flour, sifted
1 teaspoon baking powder, sifted
1 cup chopped raisins
1/2 cup nut meats

Mix spices with sugar and mix with shortening and add syrup. Mix soda with the buttermilk and add to sugar mixture. Add eggs, well beaten to sifted flour and baking powder. Add chopped raisins and nuts. Blend well. Put into 9 x 13" pan. Bake at 350 degrees for 40 minutes. Test for doneness. Cool. Frost with Penuche Frosting below.

Penuche Frosting

> 3 cups brown sugar
> 1 cup milk
> 1/2 stick of butter
> 1 teaspoon vanilla
> 1 cup nut meats for top of cake

Put sugar and milk on to boil. Stirring constantly, boil until it forms a soft ball when dropped in cold water. Remove from heat; add butter and vanilla. Beat. Cool for 10 minutes and spread before hard on spice cake.

Chocolate Spice Cake

> 1 cup sugar
> 1/2 cup shortening or lard
> 1 egg, beaten
> 1 cup sour milk
> 1 teaspoon soda
>   2 cups flour
> 1 teaspoon cinnamon
> 1/2 teaspoon cloves
> 1/2 teaspoon nutmeg
> 2 tablespoons molasses
> 2 tablespoons cocoa
> 1/2 teaspoon salt
> 1/2 cup nuts (optional)
> 1/2 cup chopped raisins (optional)

Cream sugar and shortening. Add soda to milk. Add all other ingredients in order listed. Mix well and turn out into a greased 9x13" cake pan. Add nuts and raisins if desired. Bake in 350 degree oven for 35 minutes. Check for doneness by putting a wooden toothpick into center of cake. If it comes out clean, it is done.

Jellyroll

Mother made this often, as it was a family favorite! It came from Grandmother Anastázia Cukr-Brendlová.

>4 eggs
>2/3 cup sugar
>2/3 cup flour
>1/4 teaspoon salt
>2 teaspoons baking powder
>Confectioners' sugar
>Raspberry jelly

Separate eggs. Beat egg yolks well. Add sugar, then flour, salt, and baking powder. Beat egg whites separately until they will not slide out of the bowl when tipped. Fold egg whites into batter, stirring thoroughly, each time. Spread batter into jellyroll pan that has been lined with waxed paper. Bake at 300 degrees for 15–20 minutes. Prepare tea towel dusted with confectioners' sugar. Turn cake out on towel. Sprinkle with the powdered sugar. Roll up while still warm. When cooled, unroll and spread with raspberry jelly or filling of choice. Roll up again. Sprinkle with confectioners' sugar to serve.

Nutty Cake - *Teta* Anna Mráz

>6 eggs
>1-1/2 cups sugar
>1/2 pound butter
>2 teaspoons vanilla
>1-1/2 cups flour
>2 teaspoons baking powder
>1 cup ground walnuts

Separate eggs. Beat egg whites until soft peaks form. Beat yolks until fluffy. Melt sugar and butter together. Add vanilla. Mix with beater until creamy. Add flour, baking powder and mix. Fold in yolks, then whites and add ground nuts. Mix well and pour into a greased angel food tin.

Bake in 350 degree oven for 1 hour. Don't open oven or it will fall. Let sit for about 10 minutes after taking from oven. Invert pan to cool, placing middle of the cake pan on top of large upside-down glass. When cool, run knife around inside edge of pan and tip out onto large plate. Dust with powdered sugar.

Chocolate Cake - *Teta* Emma Mráz DeFabio

1-1/2 cups sugar
1/2 cup lard or oleo
2 eggs
1/2 cup sweet milk
2 teaspoons baking soda
1 teaspoon salt
1/2 cup cocoa
2 cups flour
1 cup boiling water

Cream sugar and lard. Beat eggs and add to creamed mixture. Add milk and dry ingredients. Mix and add water a little at a time, mixing all the while. Put into small 8x8" cake pan. Bake in 350 degree oven for 20–30 minutes.

Angel Food Cake

1 cup sifted cake flour (can use regular, but best
   with cake flour)
1-1/2 cups sugar, sifted and divided
1-1/2 cups egg whites (room temperature)
1-1/2 teaspoons cream of tartar
1/2 teaspoon salt
1/2 teaspoon vanilla

Sift flour before measuring. Sift 3/4 cup sugar with the flour 4 times. Sift the other 3/4 cup of sugar and set aside. Beat egg whites with cream of tartar and salt until they don't slip in the bowl. Add the 3/4 cup sugar two tablespoons at a time, folding in. Add vanilla. Add flour and sugar mixture last, adding 2 tablespoons at a time. Fold, don't mix. When all flour mixture is folded in, put into ungreased angel food pan.

If you do not have a pan with removable bottom, place a piece of waxed paper on bottom of pan, cut into shape of tube pan and insert.

Bake at 250 or 300 degrees for 1 hour. Remove from oven and let rest for 10 minutes. Invert angel food tin over large glass for support. When cool, tip, run sharp knife around edges and center of pan, tip again onto cake plate. Loosen top by running knife under it, if necessary.

Caraway Cake - *Teta* Margaret Mráz-Maleček

> 5 eggs, separated
> 1/4 teaspoon salt
> 1-1/2 cups sugar, divided
> 1 cup butter or margarine, softened
> 1-2/3 cups cake flour
> 2 teaspoons caraway seeds
> 1 teaspoon lemon extract
> 1/4 cup confectioners' sugar for dusting

Beat egg whites and salt until foamy. Gradually beat in 1/2 cup sugar until stiff peaks form. Set aside. In another bowl, cream butter and remaining sugar until well mixed. Add egg yolks one at a time beating well. Add flour, caraway, and lemon extract. Mix well. Fold in egg whites, making sure all is blended well. Spoon into a well greased tube pan.

Bake at 300 degrees for 70 minutes. Turn out and dust with confectioners' sugar.

Creamed Cottage-Cheese Cheesecake

Teta Emma Mráz DeFabio

> 1 pound creamed cottage cheese
> 1 cup sugar
> 2 tablespoons cornstarch
> 2 tablespoons melted butter
> 3/4 cup milk
> 2 eggs, beaten

Juice of 1/2 lemon
1 teaspoon grated lemon rind
1/2 cup cooked raisins
1 teaspoon cinnamon
1 teaspoon sugar

Mix all ingredients as listed above. Set bowl aside. Make crust.

Crust

2 tablespoons butter
1 cup flour
1/2 teaspoon baking powder
1 egg, beaten
1/4 cup sugar

Mix all ingredients in order and press into 9x13" cake pan. Pour cottage cheese mixture over crust. Bake in 375 degree oven for 30–35 minutes. When wooden toothpick comes out clean, it is done.

Raw Apple Cake - *Teta* Esther Schuster-Mráz

3/4 cup brown sugar
3/4 cup white sugar
1/2 cup shortening
2 eggs, beaten
2-1/2 cups flour, sifted
1 teaspoon baking powder, sifted
1 teaspoon baking soda, sifted
1/2 teaspoon salt, sifted
1 cup cold water
2 cups sliced raw apples
1/2 cup nuts, chopped

Cream first 3 ingredients and add eggs. Sift flour, baking powder, baking soda, and salt together. Add 1 cup cold water alternately with dry ingredients to creamed mixture. Add 2 cups chopped raw apples and 1/2 cup chopped nuts. Turn out batter into 9x13" pan. Mix and sprinkle topping on cake before baking. Bake in 325–350 degree oven for 30 minutes.

Topping

2 tablespoons brown sugar
1/4 cup nuts, chopped

Buttermilk Cake
- Anne Peroutka

1/2 cup butter
1 cup sugar
2 eggs, beaten
1 teaspoon vanilla
2 cups sifted flour
1 teaspoon baking powder
1 teaspoon baking soda
1 cup buttermilk

Topping

1 cup white sugar
1/2 cup brown sugar
1 teaspoon cinnamon
1 cup chopped nuts

*Rusyny Folk Dancers,
Tucson, Arizona*

Cream butter and sugar together. Add beaten eggs and mix well. Add vanilla. Sift dry ingredients together and add to egg mixture, alternating with buttermilk until all ingredients are mixed. Put half of batter in 9x13" pan. Sprinkle 1/2 of the topping on it. Add rest of batter and sprinkle remaining topping on top. Bake at 350 degrees for 35–40 minutes. Serve with whipped cream or plain.

Orange Cake - *Teta* Margaret Mráz-Maleček

3 egg whites
1-1/4 cups granulated sugar, divided
1/3 cup cooking oil
1 whole egg
1/3 cup sour cream
1/3 cup unsweetened applesauce
1 tablespoon vanilla
1 teaspoon orange extract

2 tablespoons packed grated orange peel
1/2 cup orange juice
2-1/4 cups cake flour
1-1/8 teaspoons baking powder
1/4 teaspoon baking soda
1/2 teaspoon salt
2 tablespoons powdered sugar

Beat egg whites until foamy. Add 1/4 cup of granulated sugar, beating until whites are stiff. Set aside. Beat oil, remaining granulated sugar, whole egg, sour cream, applesauce, vanilla, orange extract, orange peel, and juice.

Mix dry ingredients, except powdered sugar, together. Gradually add flour mixture to liquid mixture a little at a time. Fold in egg whites. Mix thoroughly. Turn into greased Bundt cake pan.

Preheat oven to 350 degrees. Bake 40–45 minutes. Cool 10 minutes and remove from pan. When cool, sprinkle with powdered sugar.

Feather Basters (*Pierka*)

Most Slovak women are very frugal and rarely do they waste something that might be put to use. It was often said they used everything from a goose, but the honk! Feathers were used for two purposes: the small soft down was taken from the base of the feather and, along with smaller feathers, was used for pillows or feather "ticks." By a process of weaving with string or thick thread, the quill part of the feather was woven together to make a sturdy pastry brush. Once woven, these were washed in hot soapy water and scalded to sterilize them. They were used to baste bakery or roasts with lard or butter. After use, another hot soapy water bath was in order, along with a clear hot water rinse. They were left in the open air to dry, ready for the next use.

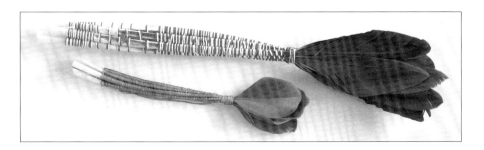

Frostings

Caramel Frosting

>2 cups brown sugar
>1 cup water
>1 tablespoon butter
>1/4 cup cream

Mix brown sugar and water. Cook to soft ball stage—when 1/2 teaspoon of mixture dropped into cold water forms a soft ball. Remove from heat, add butter. Beat until consistency desired to spread on cake. Add cream as needed to spread.

Confectioners' Frosting

>1 egg white, beaten
>1-1/4 cups confectioners' sugar
>1 teaspoon vanilla
>1 tablespoon milk

Beat egg white and add sugar. Continue to beat. Add vanilla and a bit of milk to get to spreading consistency. Can add more milk or more sugar, depending on how stiff you want the frosting.

Vanilla Butter Frosting

>1 pound confectioners' sugar, sifted
>1/2 cup butter
>1/8 teaspoon salt
>5 tablespoons milk
>2 teaspoons vanilla

Mix sugar, butter, salt, and milk together, blending after each addition. Add vanilla. Beat until creamy. Frosting covers a large cake. Refrigerate.

Teta Nettie's Chocolate Frosting

> 1/3 cup butter
> 2 squares melted bitter chocolate
> 1 teaspoon vanilla
> Powdered sugar
> 5 teaspoons cream
> 1 egg white, beaten

Cream butter with melted chocolate. Add vanilla and enough powdered sugar and cream for spreading consistency, alternating sugar and cream. Fold in 1 beaten egg white.

Seven Minute Frosting

> 2-1/4 cups sugar
> 1-1/2 tablespoons white corn syrup
> 7-1/2 tablespoons water
> 3 egg whites, beaten until stiff peaks form
> 1-1/2 teaspoons vanilla

Combine all ingredients except egg whites and vanilla in top of double boiler. Mix well. Cook over boiling water for 3 minutes. Add egg whites and vanilla. Remove from heat, but leave over hot water and beat with rotary beater 7 minutes, or until consistency to spread.

Modra plate

151

Favorite Family Desserts

Every meal ended with a dessert! Sometimes mother got creative and made things up. I remember having cooked pitted prunes, cooked apricots, or pineapple mixed in whipping cream. The whipping cream was whipped from scratch with a hand beater. Mother often added grated vanilla bean, and confectioners' sugar.

Rice Pudding

    1 cup rice, boiled in 2-1/2 cups water, drained
    1 cup milk
    1/2 cup sugar
    1 tablespoon flour
    Dash salt
    3 eggs, beaten
    1 teaspoon vanilla or almond flavoring
    1/2 cup cooked raisins
    1/2 cup cooked prunes
    3 tablespoons sugar mixed with few dashes of cinnamon

Heat milk, mix in sugar, flour, and salt. Pour into cooked rice that has been drained. Add beaten eggs, and flavoring. Add raisins, prunes, and fold together. Add cinnamon and sugar and blend well. Sprinkle more cinnamon and sugar over the top. Bake in oven for 45 minutes at 300 degrees.

Bread Pudding

    1 cup brown sugar, packed
    2 tablespoons butter
    1-1/2 cups water
    1 teaspoon ground cinnamon
    1/2 teaspoon ground nutmeg
    5 cups old bread, toasted and cut into coarse cubes
    1/2 cup chopped walnut meats
    1/2 cup raisins
    1 apple chopped fine

Heat sugar, butter, and water. Add cinnamon and nutmeg and bring to boil, stirring constantly. Simmer 5 minutes. Layer 1-1/2 cups bread cubes, nuts, raisins, and apple in ungreased casserole. Repeat layering. Pour hot liquid over top. Bake in oven for 45 minutes at 350 degrees.

Custard for Ice Cream

We used two ways to make ice cream. We used a hand crank method sometimes and, at times, the ingredients were frozen in ice cube trays. There was no such thing as an electric ice cream maker when we were growing up.

> 2-1/2 cups sugar
> 1 level tablespoon cornstarch
> 2 quarts milk
> 2 eggs, separated, yolks and whites beaten
> Pinch of salt
> 2 tablespoons vanilla
> 1 pint cream
> Rock salt and ice (see directions below)

Mix sugar and cornstarch together. Bring 2 quarts of milk to scalding in double boiler. Add 2 beaten yolks to which a pinch of salt has been added. Gradually add sugar mixture to hot milk. Add vanilla. Beat cream and add to mixture. Add 2 beaten egg whites last, folding into custard mixture. Keep stirring and cooking until mixture thickens. Cool and beat.

For crank type freezer, pour custard ingredients into clean freezer can. Put dasher in place. Cover can and adjust crank. Place can into freezer tub. Fill freezer tub 1/3 full of ice; add layer of rock salt and remaining ice alternately with layers of rock salt. (Use 6 parts ice to 1 part rock salt.) Crank until ice cream is cold and hard. Keep turning crank until it becomes almost too hard to do so. Draw off water. Remove lid and take out dasher. Push ingredients down into bottom of can with large spoon. Replace lid and repack ice and rock salt. Allow custard to sit for a few hours, and then spoon out of can. Serve.

Fresh Peach Ice Cream

2 cups peach pulp
3/4 cup sugar
Juice of 1 lemon
2 eggs, separated
2 tablespoons sugar
1/2 pint cream
Pinch of salt
1/2 teaspoon almond flavoring

Select soft peaches. Peel and mash thoroughly. Dissolve sugar in lemon juice and add to peaches. Pour into ice cube tray and freeze 45 minutes to 1 hour. Beat egg whites, adding 2 tablespoons sugar. Add yolks and mix. Whip cream to thick custard consistency. Combine with beaten eggs, adding salt and almond flavoring. Add frozen peach pulp and mix lightly. Return to freezer to freeze. When frozen, scoop out with large spoon into sauce dishes.

Shingles

4 egg yolks, beaten
3 teaspoons sugar
3 whole eggs
Splash of brandy
Dash of salt
2-1/2 cups flour
Confectioners' sugar

Mix all ingredients together, adding flour last. Beat very well. Should be a soft dough. Roll out thin, cut lengthwise, into rectangular shapes. Looks like old-fashioned shingles. Fry in deep fat. When cool, sprinkle with confectioners' sugar.

Dr. Martin Mešša photograph

Slovak bride's kroj *from Hont*

Cornstarch Pudding

    5 tablespoons cornstarch
    Scant cup sugar
    Pinch of salt
    1 quart milk
    2 eggs, beaten
    1 teaspoon vanilla

Add dry ingredients together in bowl. Put milk into pan and begin to bring to scalding. Stir constantly so it doesn't scorch. Slowly mix eggs into milk. Add dry ingredients a little at a time. Continue stirring. When well blended, allow to simmer for about 5 minutes. Cool, add 1 teaspoon vanilla. Pour into dessert dishes. Refrigerate until set.

Individual Meringues - *Teta* Esther Schuster-Mráz

    4 egg whites
    1 cup sugar
    1/2 teaspoon cream of tartar
    1/4 teaspoon vanilla
    1/2 teaspoon vinegar
    Pinch of salt
    Sweetened strawberries or raspberries
    Whipped cream

Preheat oven to 300 degrees. Beat egg whites until stiff peaks form. Gradually add sugar and cream of tartar while beating. Add vinegar, vanilla, and salt. Drop onto brown store-paper lined baking sheet. Hollow out center with back of tablespoon. A drop of food coloring makes these seasonal. Bake in 300 degree oven for 1 hour. Turn off oven and leave meringues until oven is completely cool, or may be left in oven overnight. Makes approximately 6 individual meringues. Serve sweetened strawberries or raspberries in meringues, or scoops of sherbet. Top with whipped cream.

Love Knots - *Teta* Margaret Mráz-Maleček

5 egg yolks
1/2 teaspoon salt
3 tablespoons sugar
1 tablespoon light rum
5 tablespoons sour cream
2-1/2 cups flour
Oil for frying
Confectioners' sugar

Add salt to egg yolks and beat until lemon colored. Add sugar and rum and continue to beat. Add sour cream and flour alternately, mixing well. Knead on floured board until dough blisters. Cut in half and roll dough very thin. Cut into 2 x 4-inch strips, slit center. Pull dough through slits. Fry in hot oil or fat until lightly browned. When cool, dust with powdered sugar.

Cottage Cheese Torte - *Teta* Esther Schuster-Mráz

30 graham crackers, rolled fine or
  cookie crumbs (1-1/2 cups)
1 cup sugar (scant)
1/4 cup melted butter
2 pounds cottage cheese
1 cup sugar
1/4 cup flour
1 teaspoon vanilla
5 eggs, beaten
1/2 cup milk or sweet cream
1/4 teaspoon salt
1/2 cup softened cooked raisins (optional)

Mix first 3 ingredients to make crust. Pat into 9x13" cake pan, reserving 1/4 of the crumbs for torte top. Force cottage cheese through strainer or sieve. Sift dry ingredients together and set aside. Mix vanilla, eggs, milk or cream together and mix with cottage cheese mixture. Add dry ingredients. Mix together. Add raisins, if desired. Pour into cake pan on top of crust. Cover with remaining crumbs.

Bake in oven for 15 minutes at 400 degrees. Reduce heat to moderate oven—350 degrees for another 45 minutes. Torte should be firm. Cool and cut to serve. Sprinkle with a little cinnamon and sugar, or nutmeg.

Apple Coffee Cake

> 1/3 cup raisins
> 1 cup butter or margarine
> 1 cup sugar
> 3 large eggs
> 1 cup dairy sour cream
> 1 teaspoon vanilla
> 2-1/2 cups sifted all-purpose flour
> 2 teaspoons baking powder
> 1 teaspoon baking soda
> 1/2 teaspoon salt
> 1 jar or can apple filling
> 1-1/4 teaspoons cinnamon
> 1/2 cup firmly packed brown sugar
> 1/2 cup finely chopped nuts

Simmer raisins for few minutes to plump up before using. Drain. Grease 9x13" cake pan. Cream butter and sugar thoroughly. Add eggs one at a time, beating well after each addition. Mix in sour cream and vanilla. Blend. Combine flour, baking powder, soda, and salt. Stir into creamed mixture. Spread half of batter into prepared pan. Spread with apple filling and then raisins. Cover with remaining batter. Combine cinnamon, brown sugar, and nuts. Sprinkle over top of batter. Bake at 375 degrees for 30 minutes. Cool and cut into squares before serving.

Christmas Holidays

Great preparations were made for the Christmas season in the Brendel household. For weeks, anticipation mounted and good cheer was evident in the cleaning, shopping, wrapping, decorating, baking, and cooking chores. The house was in order and picture perfect. The tradition of decorating the tree on Christmas Eve day was changed in our family, and everyone took part in its trimming several days before Christmas.

A few days before Christmas, the activity shifted exclusively to the kitchen. The rest of the house was quiet—tree trimmed and decorations fixed. Along with fresh pine scent, wonderful aromas filled the air, and the spirit of Christmas was upon us. It was a happy time and one of great expectation.

Christmas Eve day, late in the afternoon, the table was set with Grandma's finest European china. A fine white linen tablecloth, monogrammed with her initials, AB, and matching napkins were laid out. The beautiful rose embossed soup terrine with matching bowl and platter were taken from the china cabinet and washed in readiness to be filled with special foods.

Although we had no source for straw, my mother told me when she was a child they would bring straw into their home and spread it near the table

Slovak Cornhusk Nativity

as a reminder that Christ was born in a stable and laid on straw in the manger. Another custom shared was that an empty chair and plate were left at the table to remember someone who had died that year or to welcome an extra person, if someone should come unexpectedly.

We dressed in our finest clothing for this special occasion. Mother was an excellent seamstress so, as we were growing up, we had new outfits for holidays. Christmas was extra special. We dressed up for church and kept our good clothing on for the family celebration. Members of our family were churchgoers and always attended church services in the late afternoon. As years went by, some attended the late candlelight service. Our home celebration was arranged around the services since we had church musicians involved, sometimes at both services. When the family attended services in the late afternoon, we frequently brought elderly people home with us to share our Christmas Eve celebration. After church, we enjoyed our traditional meal and then opened gifts. There were small gifts under the tree for our visitors, and mother always sent food home with them to enjoy the next day. As I think back, I realize we were taught by example two valuable lessons: to reach out in love, to share what we had.

Tradition in the Slovak home dictated the absence of meat for many years. Although it is noted that carp was originally used in the main dish for our Christmas Eve dinner, it was replaced with veal and then pork as years went by.

Santa Claus came to our home during the night. We left milk and cookies for him and his elves and often remarked it was no small wonder Santa was fat!

Teta Anna and *Bobaľky*

Teta Anna told me they used to have *Bobaľky* on Christmas Eve. She said her mother "stole" sweet dough from other bakery that she was making, and formed it into small balls. They were baked in the oven, and when done were put into a bowl and served with poppy seed, milk, and honey.

With the mention of poppy seed, she told of an old pagan superstition. Raw poppy seed was tossed outside the door of Slovak homes so that evil spirits would be challenged with picking up each and every seed. Once busy doing so, they no longer considered entering the house to cast an evil spell on the household. Meant to be serious, the thought of it made me laugh! The honey served on Christmas Eve *oplátka* (wafers) was significant because it had biblical connections. My mother told of days when her own mother would give each of the family members an *oplátka* on which honey was drizzled, as a reminder to keep Christ in their lives during the coming year. This was a part of their Christmas Eve tradition.

Christmas Day was a day to enjoy family and friends. In the morning, we were allowed to visit our neighbors, the Peroutka family, to see what gifts Santa left behind and possibly play a new board game or try out a new toy. The early part of the afternoon was spent at home and, later in the day, we went to enjoy another Christmas feast with family who lived nearby and to wish them a *Veselé Vianoce a Šťastlivý Nový Rok!* (Merry Christmas and a Happy New Year!)

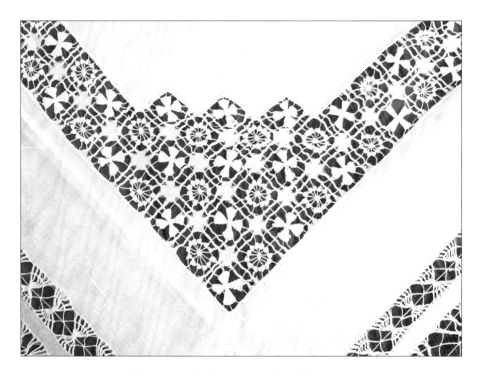

Beautiful cutwork from Grandmother Anna Mráz

Traditional Slovak Christmas Eve Recipes

Breaded Veal or Pork Chops

> 14 lean pork chops or veal steaks (I've used both
> depending on availability)
> 2 cups flour or buttermilk pancake mix
> 1 teaspoon seasoned salt
> 1 teaspoon paprika
> 1 teaspoon garlic salt
> 4 eggs, beaten
> 1/2 cup milk
> 4 cups coarsely ground soda crackers
> 1 cup of cooking oil, more if needed

Preheat oven to 300 degrees. Blend pancake mix or flour, with seasonings, in large bowl. Coat meat with mixture. (Shake in large plastic bag, if desired.) When coated, set on large platters. Dip each piece of meat into egg mixture. Coat with cracker crumbs. Brown in heated oil in frying pans. (I use 2 pans at the same time.) When brown, transfer meat into large 9x13" cake pans. (I use 4 of them.) Don't layer. Cover with aluminum foil. Bake in preheated oven for 45 minutes and then turn oven down to 200 degrees while attending church service. As soon as you get home, remove foil and, if necessary, turn up oven so meat browns and crisps up.

Carp, Veal, or Pork Loin in Black Gravy

> 1 large carp cut into pieces, or 1-1/2 to 2 pounds veal, or
> 1-1/2 to 2 pounds pork loin (see directions)
> 2 carrots cut into 1/2-inch pieces
> 3/4 cup whole celery root (inside of celery stalk), diced
> 2 tablespoons of jellied cranberry sauce or raspberry jelly
> 12 whole walnut meats
> 15 blanched almonds
> 1/2 cup white raisins
> 1/2 cup dark raisins
> 12 plump prunes with pits
> 1/2 bag of ginger snaps

This recipe was originally made with traditional Slavic Christmas carp. The story goes: grandma didn't care for carp so she substituted it with veal. Veal became hard to get and, even if available, was very costly. Grandma settled for pork. So did we.

Since there are other traditional entrées served in our home on Christmas Eve and Christmas Day, about 2 pounds of pork loin is enough. Cut up meat of choice into about 6–8 good-sized chunks. Simmer in water, enough to cover, for 30–45 minutes, depending on tenderness of the meat.

Add carrots first, then add celery, jelly, walnuts, and raisins. For celery root, I use inside "heart" of the celery stalks, as I've never found celery root at any market. Test carrots as they take longest to cook. They should be a bit crisp. Add prunes last. Simmer about 5 more minutes. Do not overcook as prunes become mushy. Prunes are not pitted because the number of pits left on a young man's plate signifies the number of girlfriends he will have!

Add ginger snaps to thicken gravy to desired consistency. I use about 3 cups of ginger snaps, but my mother used less. If gravy gets too thick, add water. Serve over sliced bread dumplings.

Note: In Slovakia, live carp is sold on street corners during the holiday seasons. People take the fish home and keep it alive in a bathtub until it is time to cook it on Christmas Eve.

Bread Dumplings

> 2 tablespoons butter
> 2 slices bread, cubed
> 2 cups flour
> 2 teaspoons baking powder
> 1 teaspoon salt
> 2 eggs
> 1/2 cup milk

Cube bread and brown in butter, stirring with wooden spoon. Set aside. Mix flour, baking powder, and salt in deep bowl. Add cubed bread. Beat eggs and milk together. Pour over flour mixture and mix together.

Cover with clean towel and let rest for at least 1/2 hour, preferably 1 hour. Dough will be sticky. Turn out onto floured bread board. Sift extra flour onto the dough so you can work with it. Form long roll and cut in two. Drop 2 logs into large pot of boiling water. Make certain pot is large enough so dumplings have room to "swim."

Do not remove cover while cooking. Turn down heat as water comes to a boil. Cook 15 minutes. Take out with slotted spoon and put on platter. Slice with 15-inch length of store string or thread, laying dumpling on string, and with two hands pulling string up to cross at top. It is pulled through the dumpling, making nice slices. Layer on platter and drizzle with butter. Sprinkle with paprika before serving. Makes 6 good-sized slices of dumplings. I triple the batch for Christmas Eve.

Grandma's Potato Salad

> 6 pounds potatoes (I cook one potato per person and
> a few extra for good measure!)
> 6 eggs
> 1 generous cup diced onion
> 1 generous cup diced celery
> 1 16 ounce carton cultured sour cream
> 1/2 teaspoon celery salt
> Salt, pepper, and paprika

Cook potatoes, cool and slice into large mixing bowl. For better flavor, and added food value, scrub and cook potatoes in their jackets. Cool, peel, and cut up. Cook eggs. Bring to boil, turn off heat and set timer for 15 minutes. (Mother said if you overcook eggs, they turn green. They do!) Cool, peel, and slice eggs into small pieces into separate bowl. Add onions and celery.

Layer the ingredients, potatoes, eggs, diced items, salt and pepper, and a little of the sour cream, then another layer, so you don't break the ingredients too much when stirring. Add balance of sour cream. With large spoon, gently lift from bottom, blending ingredients together. Cover and refrigerate overnight. Garnish with generous amount of paprika before serving. Serves 14 people.

Teta Nettie's Sausage/Kidney Bean/ Sauerkraut Dish

This is served on Christmas Day with rye bread. I took my mother to an annual Lugerville School picnic pot luck one year and brought this dish. An older woman came to me and said she knew what dish we brought because Nettie Mráz was the only woman she knew who put kidney beans in her sauerkraut!

> 2 rings of kielbasa (Polish sausage)
> 2 large cans or jars of sauerkraut
> 1 large can kidney beans, drained (or soak dry
>   kidney beans overnight and cook until tender)
> 2 large cans button mushrooms
>   (or 3 cups of dried mushrooms)
> 1 large onion, diced
> 1/4 cup sweet butter
> 2 tablespoons flour (for browning)

Simmer kielbasa after cutting into pieces, and drain for a healthier dish. Rinse sauerkraut. Place in kettle, add enough water to cover. Simmer about 1/2 hour.

Brown onion in butter and add flour to make *zápražka* (browned flour or roux). When very dark, add water, stirring constantly to make a thickening sauce. Add to sauerkraut and continue cooking on low heat. Add kielbasa, button mushrooms, and lastly, kidney beans. Heat through and serve. This dish can be made a few days before and refrigerated. It keeps very well.

I remember my mother picking wild mushrooms in the woods not far from home. She dried them in the "back room kitchen." She threaded a needle, ran it through a few mushrooms at a time, and hung them over the clothesline to dry. She mailed them to *Teta* Nettie in California so she could make this dish for her family with "real" mushrooms as a surprise!

Apple Strudel

1-1/2 teaspoons salad oil
1 small whole egg, unbeaten
3/4 cup lukewarm water
2-1/3 cups sifted flour
1 cup cooled butter or margarine, melted
Confectioners' sugar

Apple Filling:

1 cup crushed vanilla wafers
  (or saved cookie crumbs), divided
1/4 teaspoon each of nutmeg and cinnamon
2-1/2 pounds fresh apples, pared and sliced
1 tablespoon grated lemon rind
1/2 cup light raisins
3/4 cup walnut pieces, not chopped

Preparation: use kitchen table as work station. Spread out clean white tablecloth. Flour lightly, enough so dough won't stick to cloth. Good idea to remove rings so dough doesn't get torn by them. Heat oven to 375 degrees.

Combine oil, egg, water and, using fork, beat until smooth. Measure flour into large bowl, make well in center. Pour in oil mixture and stir to make soft dough. Turn dough onto lightly floured surface. Working with dough: throw dough down hard on table about 100 times, kneading until dough is smooth. Lightly brush dough with melted butter. Put an inverted bowl over dough and let rest in a warm place for 30 minutes. Put dough in center of cloth. With floured rolling pin, roll dough into large square, about 16x16 inches. Using fingers, lightly brush entire surface with melted butter. With buttered hands underneath it, with a pulling motion, gently stretch dough toward table edge about 20–24 inches. Lift carefully to avoid tearing it. This takes patience and can't be hurried. When dough is stretched so it hangs over table and is thin enough to see through, snip off any thick edges with kitchen shears. Let dough dry a little before next step, about 15 minutes will do. When strudel dough is manageable, sprinkle lightly again with melted butter. Add apple filling.

Filling:

Beginning with the edge closest to you and in a row no more than 5 inches out from you, sprinkle the entire length of the dough, left to right, with 1/2 of the vanilla wafers, nutmeg, and cinnamon. Toss apples with lemon rind, raisins, and nuts. Add balance of vanilla wafer mixture to top of apples. Begin to roll up jellyroll fashion, lifting cloth from underneath to roll it along. Turn in extra dough on edges, over the filling, when rolling. It is easier to roll. With a sharp knife, cut roll exactly in half, and again using the floured cloth, ease roll to the edge of the table onto greased cookie sheet or jellyroll pan, one at a time. Use broad spatula if needed to help. Bend strudel into half moon shape. Close up open end. Brush with melted butter. Bake 55–60 minutes or until crisp and lightly browned. Serve warm. Sprinkle with confectioners' sugar. Makes 2 strudels. About 8 servings each.

Note: See *Houska* or Christmas Bread on page 101.

Cranberry Pudding

> 1-1/3 cups flour
> 1/2 teaspoon salt
> 1 teaspoon baking soda
> 1/4 teaspoon cinnamon
> 1/4 teaspoon cloves
> 1/4 teaspoon mace
> 2 cups coarsely chopped cranberries
> 1/3 cup hot water
> 1/2 cup light molasses

Sift dry ingredients together and mix well. Add cranberries. Add water and molasses together and mix well. Grease generously 1 pound pudding mold or 1 pound coffee can and fill with batter. Place covered mold or can into large pot filled with 2 inches of water. Cover pot and bring to boil. Reduce heat to simmer and steam for 2 hours. Wait for 10 minutes, then loosen edges with a sharp knife. Invert and put pudding on a plate. It may be cut into wedges, or served by spoonfuls. Serve with hot butter sauce.

Hot Butter Sauce

 1 cup sugar
 1 cup cream or milk
 1/2 cup butter
 1/2 cup rum (optional)

Mix altogether and put into double boiler. Keep stirring until well blended and almost boiling. Serve warm over pudding. Serves 8 people. This is very rich.

Cookies

It became a tradition to have my two granddaughters bake Christmas cookies with me prior to the holiday season. Most every year since they were quite small, we were able to do this. We baked 16 different kinds of cookies. Since my daughters and daughter-in-law all work outside the home, they welcomed the sight of trays full of cookies for the holidays.

Rakvičky (Coffin Cookies)

 3-1/2 cups flour
 1-3/4 cups granulated sugar
 7 ounces ground walnuts
   (just short of one cup)
 Scant 2 cups and scant
   1/4 cup sweet butter
 2 whole eggs

Coffin Tins

Small coffin-shaped cookie molds may be found in kitchen specialty shops. Grease and flour cookie forms.

Mix ingredients together thoroughly, taking about 15 minutes. Press into bottom and sides of form, about 2/3 full to form a coffin look. Bake in 375 degree oven for 10 minutes, then bake at 325 degrees for an additional 20 minutes.

Let cookies cool and either flip out pushing bottom and sides of form, or use sharp knife around edges to pop out. Put them right side up on tray and fill with butter filling.

Butter Filling

    1 pound sweet butter (softened)
    1 egg yolk, beaten
    1 shot rum
    2 tablespoons confectioners' sugar (to start)

Cream first three ingredients together. Begin with 2 tablespoons of confectioners' sugar, adding a little at a time to get desired consistency to easily fill coffin crusts. Let set in cool place before adding glaze.

Glaze

    Juice of one whole lemon
    1 tablespoon powdered sugar (to start)
    1 tablespoon hot water

Mix well and frost cooled coffins. Refrigerate until use.

Ginger Creams

    1 cup shortening
    1 cup brown sugar, packed
    1/2 cup molasses
    1 cup sour milk or cream
    3 teaspoons baking soda
    1 teaspoon cinnamon
    4 cups flour
    1 teaspoon ginger
    2 eggs, beaten
    1/2 teaspoon salt
    1 teaspoon vanilla

Cream shortening and brown sugar. Add molasses. Mix well. Add eggs and mix well. Combine flour and all other dry ingredients, then add a little at a time to liquid mixture. Keep adding until all ingredients are included. Drop by spoonfuls 2 inches apart on ungreased cookie sheet. Bake in 375 degree oven for 10 minutes. Cool and frost with vanilla butter frosting.

Vanilla Butter Frosting

1/2 cup butter, softened
3 cups powdered sugar
1-1/2 teaspoons vanilla
2 tablespoons milk (approximately)

Blend butter and sugar. Stir in milk and vanilla. Beat until smooth. If too thick, add a little more milk. This recipe will frost all of the ginger creams. Frosting enough to frost two 8 inch layers, or a 13x9" inch cake.

Butter Cookies

1/2 pound butter, softened
1/2 pound (1-2/3 cups) powdered sugar
2 eggs
1/2 teaspoon baking soda
1/2 teaspoon salt
1/2 teaspoon vanilla or almond extract
3-1/2 cups flour

Mix all ingredients together in order listed. Roll out and cut cookies with a glass or cookie cutters or use in cookie press. Bake in 300 degree oven approximately 8–10 minutes until lightly brown.

Sour Cream Roll Outs

1-1/2 cups sugar
1/2 cup shortening
2 eggs, beaten
1 cup sour milk or cream
1 teaspoon vanilla
2-3/4 cups sifted flour
1/2 teaspoon baking powder
1/2 teaspoon baking soda
1/2 teaspoon salt

Cream shortening and sugar. Add eggs. Beat well. Add sour cream and vanilla. In separate bowl, blend flour, baking powder, baking soda, salt. Add 1/4 of flour mixture at a time to first mixture. Stir well after each addition. When flour is used up, you should have a stiff dough. Chill for easier handling. Take 1/4 of the dough out at a time, roll out and cut into circles. Bake in 350 degree oven for 8–10 minutes or until brown on edges. Frost with Vanilla Butter Frosting (see page 169) using grated vanilla bean for flavoring.

Grandma's Raisin Cookies

    2 cups raisins
    1-1/2 cups water
    2 cups brown sugar (packed)
    1 cup shortening
    3 eggs, beaten
    4 cups flour
    1 teaspoon baking soda
    1 teaspoon baking powder
    1 tablespoon cinnamon
    1 teaspoon cloves
    1/2 teaspoon allspice

Rinse and simmer raisins in water, enough to soften. Set aside. Add 1 teaspoon soda to raisin mixture. Cream brown sugar and shortening, and mix in 3 beaten eggs. Blend together all dry ingredients and sift together with flour. Do not drain, but add raisin mixture to other ingredients. Mix well. Drop by tablespoonfuls onto greased cookie sheet. Bake in 375 degree oven 10–12 minutes until brown around edges. Frost with confectioners' sugar frosting while still warm.

Powdered Sugar Frosting

    1 cup powdered sugar
    1/2 teaspoon vanilla
    Enough milk to make a good spreading consistency
        (start with 2 tablespoons)

Mix ingredients well. Add small amount of milk if needed.

Old-fashioned Chocolate Sour Cream Drops

1/2 cup soft shortening
1-1/2 cups sugar
2 eggs
2 ounces (2 squares) unsweetened chocolate, melted
1 cup thick sour cream
1 teaspoon vanilla
2-3/4 cups flour, sifted
1/2 teaspoon baking soda
1/2 teaspoon baking powder
1/2 teaspoon salt
1 cup nuts, chopped

Mix shortening, sugar, and eggs thoroughly. Add melted chocolate. Stir in sour cream and vanilla. Sift flour, baking soda, baking powder, and salt together and stir into first mixture. Add chopped nuts. Chill at least one hour. Drop rounded teaspoonfuls about two inches apart on lightly greased baking sheet. Bake in 425 degree oven 8–10 minutes or until delicately browned. Frost cooled cookies with chocolate icing. Yields about five dozen 1-1/2 inch cookies.

Chocolate Icing

1 tablespoon butter
1 ounce (1 square) unsweetened chocolate
3 tablespoons top cream or milk (I use skim!)
1-1/2 cups sifted confectioners' sugar
Cream, enough to make desired consistency

Melt butter and chocolate together over hot water. Stir in top milk and sugar. Thin with cream to make glossy and easy to spread.

Note: Top with a walnut or half a maraschino cherry. I make these smaller and pile a lot of frosting on them, then top with red and green cherry halves to add color to the Christmas cookie tray.

Moravian Stars

1 cup shortening
1 cup granulated sugar
1 cup molasses
1 egg, beaten
5 cups flour
2 teaspoons ground ginger
1 teaspoon cardamom
1-1/2 teaspoons baking soda
1 teaspoon ground cinnamon
1 teaspoon ground cloves
1/2 teaspoon salt
Colored sugar for sprinkling

Cream shortening and sugar. Beat in molasses and egg. Mix flour with ginger, cardamom, soda, cinnamon, cloves, and salt. Blend into batter. Chill overnight. Use 1/3 of dough at a time, keeping other chilled. Roll dough out on lightly floured board. Cut into different-sized stars. Place 1 inch apart on cookie sheet. Sprinkle with colored sugar before baking. Bake in 375 degree oven 8 minutes. Yields about 5 dozen depending on size of cookie cutter.

Nut Crescents

1 cup butter or margarine, softened
1/3 cup sugar
1 teaspoon almond flavoring
1 tablespoon water
2 cups sifted flour
1/2 cup chopped almonds
Sifted confectioners' sugar

Cream first 4 ingredients together. Stir in flour and almonds. Mix well and shape into pencil thin crescents. Place on ungreased cookie sheet. Bake in 350 degree oven 15–20 minutes but watch so cookies don't get too brown. Cool. Roll in powdered sugar. Yields 60 cookies.

Best Gingersnaps

1 cup brown sugar, packed
3/4 cup cooking oil
1/4 cup dark molasses
1 egg, beaten
2 cups flour
2 teaspoons baking soda
1 teaspoon ground cinnamon
1 teaspoon ground ginger
1/2 teaspoon ground cloves
1/4 teaspoon salt
Granulated sugar for coating

Combine first 4 ingredients. Combine dry ingredients and gradually blend into molasses mixture. Form into 1-1/4 inch balls. Roll in granulated sugar. Place 2 inches apart on greased cookie sheet. Bake in 375 degree oven 10–12 minutes. Yields approximately 4 dozen.

Note: If a smaller, daintier cookie is desired, use only a teaspoon of dough for each cookie. I make them smaller at Christmas time.

Basic Spritz and Chocolate Spritz

1 cup butter, softened
1/2 cup sugar
2-1/4 cups flour
1/2 teaspoon salt
1 egg, beaten
1 teaspoon flavoring of choice
Several drops of food coloring or
2 ounces melted unsweetened chocolate
   for chocolate spritz

Cream butter and sugar. Stir in remaining ingredients one at a time. Add chocolate to the mixture for chocolate spritz. Fill spritz cookie press with roll of dough each time. Press on ungreased cookie sheets. Bake in 350 degree oven 8–10 minutes. Yields approximately 5 dozen cookies.

Lemon-Cheese Spritz

1 cup butter, softened
1 (3-ounce) package cream cheese, softened
1 cup sugar
1 egg yolk, beaten
1 teaspoon lemon extract
1 teaspoon grated lemon rind
1-1/2 cups plus 1 tablespoon flour, sifted
1/2 teaspoon salt
3 drops yellow food coloring
Yellow colored sugar, enough to sprinkle on tops

Cream butter, cream cheese, and sugar; add egg yolk and lemon extract and rind. Beat until well blended. Add sifted flour, with salt, a little at a time. Mix well. Using flower pattern, put small roll of dough into spritz cookie press. Force onto cold, ungreased cookie sheets. Sprinkle yellow sugar on top. Bake in 350 degree oven for 8–10 minutes.

Lemon Melt-Aways

1/2 cup butter, softened
2/3 cup granulated sugar
1 rind of lemon, grated
1 egg, beaten
4 tablespoons lemon juice
3 drops of yellow food coloring
2-1/2 cups flour, sifted
1 teaspoon baking powder, sifted
1 tablespoon milk
1/2 cup confectioners' sugar, sifted

Cream together butter, sugar, and lemon rind. Add beaten egg and lemon juice, food coloring, beating well after each addition. Sift flour and baking powder into creamed mixture. Blend well. Add milk, mixing altogether. Turn dough out onto lightly floured board. Roll into 50 small balls. Roll each ball with hands into sausage shape. Make an "S" shape or small logs. Place on lightly-greased cookie sheets. Bake at 325 degrees for 15–20 minutes. Cool completely and sprinkle with powdered sugar. Store in airtight container. Freezes well.

Lemon Dewdrops

1 cup butter, softened
1/2 cup confectioners' sugar
1 teaspoon real lemon juice or lemon extract
2 drops yellow food coloring
2 cups flour
1/4 teaspoon salt

Blend butter with sugar, lemon juice or extract and food coloring. Mix in flour and salt. Chill dough. Shape small balls between palms, measuring by teaspoonfuls. Place cookies 1 inch apart on ungreased cookie sheet.

Flatten ball with bottom of small juice glass, dipping in granulated sugar, if sticky. Bake at 350 degrees for 10 minutes or until set. Do not allow to brown too much. Fill with lemon filling to make a sandwich cookie with two cookies.

Lemon Filling

1/2 cup granulated sugar
2 tablespoons cornstarch
1/8 teaspoon salt
1/2 cup water
3 tablespoons lemon juice
1 tablespoon butter
2 tablespoons grated lemon peel
4 drops yellow food coloring
Confectioners' sugar for coating

Put sugar, cornstarch, and salt into small pan. Stir in water to dissolve sugar. Add lemon juice. Cook over low heat until mixture thickens, stirring constantly. Remove from heat. Stir in butter, lemon peel, and food coloring. Cool and spoon onto underside of cookie, covering it with another of the same size to make sandwich cookie. When set, roll in powdered sugar.

Note: Be sure to store these in their own tin. If stored with other cookies they become soft.

Butter Melt-Aways

1 cup butter (don't substitute)
2 cups confectioners' sugar, divided
2 teaspoons almond flavoring
2 cups flour
1/4 cup cornstarch
1/8 teaspoon salt

In large bowl mix butter and 1 cup sugar until creamy. Add almond extract. Blend well. Mix together flour, cornstarch, and salt in separate bowl. Add to first mixture and mix well. Cover bowl and chill for at least 1 hour or until easy to handle. Shape dough by heaping teaspoons into 1-inch balls. Place balls 1 inch apart on ungreased cookie sheets.

Bake in 325 degree oven for 20 minutes. Bake until set and lightly golden around edges. Cool. Sift remaining sugar into bowl. While still warm roll cookies in confectioners' sugar. Cool completely. Roll in sugar again. May add chopped almonds to dough, and form dough into crescent shapes.

Note: May use vanilla or any other extract. I use black walnut extract and chopped walnuts at times.

Pecan Butter Balls

1 cup butter, softened
1/4 cup granulated sugar
2 teaspoons vanilla extract
2 cups flour
1/2 teaspoon salt
2 cups pecans finely chopped

Mix butter with sugar and vanilla. Add flour, salt, and pecans. With wooden spoon, mix well. Shape into 1-inch balls and put on ungreased cookie sheets. Bake at 325 degrees 25 minutes or until lightly browned. Yields about 4-1/2 dozen. May freeze in airtight container.

Never-fail Christmas Cookies

1 cup margarine (butter or lard can be used)
1 cup sugar
2 eggs, beaten
4 tablespoons milk
1 teaspoon vanilla
3 cups flour
1/2 teaspoon salt
2 teaspoons baking powder
1 teaspoon baking soda
Flour for dusting cutting board

Cream margarine and sugar; add eggs, milk, and vanilla. Beat well. Mix flour, salt, baking powder, and baking soda and gradually add to first mixture. Knead lightly on floured board. Let set in bowl and cover tightly. Refrigerate overnight. Put 1/3 of dough onto floured board and roll out and cut into desired shapes with cookie cutters. Bake in 350 degree oven 10 minutes or until set.

Frost with either vanilla butter frosting (see page 169) or powdered sugar frosting (see page 170). Add 1 teaspoon of light Karo® syrup. This makes a glazed frosting and dries on cookie. Divide frosting into thirds, putting each into small bowl. Add food coloring to suit needs: green for Christmas trees, wreaths, etc.

Caramel Balls

1 cup butter
3/4 cup packed dark brown sugar
1 teaspoon maple extract
1/2 cup pecans, chopped fine
2-1/2 cups flour
1/2 teaspoon baking powder
1 cup caramel pieces
3/4 cup pistachio nuts, chopped very fine

Melt butter. Stir in sugar, maple extract, and pecans. Sift dry ingredients into butter mixture. Mix. Form balls, using rounded teaspoon. Place on ungreased cookie sheet, one inch apart. Pinch top of ball to bring to peak. Bake in 350 degree oven for 15 minutes.

While cookies cool, melt caramels over hot water. Dip flat ends of cookies into caramel. Quickly dip into pistachio nuts. Completely cover or caramel will be sticky. Yields 3-1/2 dozen.

Christmas Butter Cookies

> 1 cup soft butter (do not substitute)
> 1 cup confectioners' sugar, sifted
> 1 unbeaten egg
> 1 teaspoon vanilla
> 2-1/4 cups flour
> 1 cup candied mixed citron, minced fine
> 1-1/2 cups walnuts or pecans, chopped very fine

Mix first five ingredients in order and mix well. Add candied citron and nuts. Be sure to chop these additions very fine, otherwise you do not get clean-cut slices. Sprinkle board with powdered sugar and roll dough into three logs. Wrap in waxed paper for easier handling. Chill. Remove one roll at a time from refrigerator. Roll the log in powdered sugar again before slicing. Slice about 1/8 inch thick with very sharp knife. Lay on ungreased cookie sheet. Bake in 325 degree oven for 10 minutes. Cookie should not brown around edges. Remove from sheet after they cool. This is a very rich cookie. It does not spread while baking. Freeze to store and use as needed.

All Slovakian cornhusk dolls shown in this book are from the collection of Joan Liffring-Zug Bourret, publisher. Several poignantly depict womens' work in the rural Slovakia of yesterday.

Out of the Ordinary

There were many items in my mother's recipe box that one could say were familiar, but out of the ordinary. For instance, vast amounts of sauerkraut were made and consumed in the homes of my grandparents and parents. My uncle John recollected how my grandmother would get him and his sister Emma into the summer kitchen, scrub their feet with a scrub brush and lye soap, rinse them well, and lift them into a huge crock of sauerkraut to stomp it down. He reminisced how their feet were shriveled up from the salt brine before they were to be rescued from it. Knowing all of this, one can be thankful it now comes in cans.

Then there were the organ meat recipes. Not for the faint of heart by any means! How to pickle tongue is possibly not something the modern day housewife would need nor want to know about. Curing one hundred pounds of ham using eight pounds of salt, two pounds of brown sugar, and two ounces of saltpeter possibly wouldn't appeal to many today either, when one can go and pick up one of those succulent precooked meats in the local supermarket. Bologna sausage anyone? Taking one pint of pig meat, lean and fat? Probably not. This was something one had to wait for, as it took from ten days to two weeks in the smoke house before it was ready for consumption. This would never do in today's "life in the fast lane" society. (As the recipe reads, it got better with age!)

Meat on the farm and use of cheaper cuts of meat may speak to some of us, but not all. Again, a time frame is involved with long, slow cooking involved, as well as the addition of acid (vinegar or lemon juice), grinding, and pounding.

How to boil rice isn't even an issue anymore since the advent of dehydrated rice. Who would have guessed that it was once an art form?

And coloring for gravies and sauces doesn't belong in the "need to know" column either, as it is readily available in a bottle these days.

How about a recipe for curing one hundred pounds of beef? Anyone? Maybe not for a modern day family of four.

Lastly, and of great importance in my mother's time was Soapy Sam's lye soap recipe. For many years, the women at St. John Lutheran Church, in Phillips, Wisconsin, met during the winter months to make lye soap to send overseas. Mother was part of that group. With donated fat from trappers and farmers, the women toughed it out in the church kitchen straining and stirring a mix of ammonia, borax, and lye. With benevolent hearts and a waft of kindness as strong as the brew itself, the women lovingly cut, packed, and sent it off to Lutheran World Relief and World Missions. This recipe to end all recipes seems like a fitting end to my mother's collection.

Soapy Sam's crew made 3,000 bars of soap annually, and it was sent through Lutheran World Relief to Lutheran missions in Africa, as well as declared disaster areas in the United States. From 1967 through 1978, 34,000 bars were made and shipped. This is their recipe from Soapy Sam Samuel, the Chief.

Soapy Sam's Lye Soap

5 pounds clean strained grease
1 quart (1 can) lye
Cold water (according to directions on lye)
1 teaspoon salt
1/4 cup ammonia
2 tablespoons sugar
1/2 cup borax in 1/2 cup cold water

Cook outside if possible. In large kettle (canning kettle works well) place grease. Dissolve lye in cold water, adding slowly. Stir constantly. Add to melted grease. Stir for at least 1-1/2 hours. Add salt. Add ammonia and keep stirring. Add sugar. Cook mixture until it begins to harden, stirring constantly. Add borax. Stir until thick. Pour into shallow waxed-paper-lined boxes. When completely hardened, cut into bars, or break into pieces. This process may take several days.

Used at the turn of the century and beyond, splash cloths were in Slovak American homes behind the wash basin or dry sink to protect the walls from splashes. Maxims and folk figures were embroidered on the cloths to decorate the Slovak kitchen. Translation: "I am a little hunter."

Christianity in Slovakia

Although predominantly Roman Catholic through the ages, some interesting facts remain as remnants of Slovakia's religious past.

The Eastern Orthodox Church refers to itself as "The Church," as its roots are in Jerusalem. The twenty-first century finds the laws governing this church and its holy traditions unchanged in Slovakia, and today there are approximately seventy-thousand Orthodox believers. Since the Velvet Divorce there are administrative headquarters both in Prague, Czech Republic, and Prešov, Slovakia.

The Roman Catholic Church was introduced to the Slovak people in the ninth century and continues as the country's dominant religion today. As of 2007, there were twelve dioceses of the Roman Catholic faith operating within Slovakia. The dioceses provides priests and other clergy to minister to the large population of Catholics who clung to their faith during forty years of Communist rule. Each small village has its own church, but many parishioners travel to larger churches for worship. The priests, along with specially trained lay people, minister to the large faction of Catholics in the country.

The Communist regime transferred all Greek Catholic Church (also referred to as Byzantine Catholic Church) parishes to Russian Orthodox churches in the 1950s. Most seminarians, nuns, monks, and priests were jailed and the Pope was considered an enemy of the state. In 1968, during the Prague Spring, the Greek Catholic Church was restored and is now active once more providing services to its members.

The Baptist Church began to appear in Slovakia between 1530–1540. It was all but annihilated during the religious persecution by the Hapsburg rulers. In 1886, a group began to meet for Bible reading and, by 1888, had established a church. Other churches began before 1900, and an independent Slovak Baptist Union was formed in 1914 with four churches participating. With help from abroad, a seminary opened in Prague and four more churches were built. A mission outreach program was established for the Jewish community in 1924, but closed by the Fascist government in 1939. After World War II, new churches were built to accommodate the refugee population, as many were Slovak Baptists. In 1948, a new wave of persecution began, and, from 1949 until 1954, many churches were closed. In 1989, there were nine Baptist churches in Slovakia, and in 2007 there were twenty. In 1995, the Slovak Baptist Union signed a partnership with Southern Baptists of Virginia, USA, and the International Mission Board of the Southern Baptist Convention pledged to make the gospel known throughout Slovakia.

The Evangelical Church of the Augsburg Confession dates back to the sixteenth century Reformation and continues as a strong and growing church. With the ideas of Martin Luther permeating the countryside of Hungary, by 1670 most of the citizens of Hungary were Lutherans. The Edict of Toleration ensured religious freedom to all non-Catholics. Until 1918, Slovak Lutherans were part of the Evangelical Church in the Kingdom of Hungary, and, in 1921, the Evangelical Church of the Augsburg Confession was formed. In 2007, there were 326 congregations in fourteen conferences and an East and West district. They support all levels of education, and a school for deaf and blind children is part of the school system in Červenica. Retirement homes, social services, and special needs children are assisted by Lutheran programs, and Comenius University in Bratislava provides theological education to those who seek it.

While Martin Luther's reforms ran rampant amidst Slovaks and Germans, by 1613 John Calvin's reforms were widely accepted among the Hungarians. The formal name for a Calvinist church is Reformed Christian Church in Slovakia. While the Hungarian minority makes up most of its membership today, there are still some Slovak members.

With beginnings in the first half of the eighteenth century in England, John Wesley's beliefs were brought to Slovakia by missionaries. Wesley considered himself an Anglican minister, but the Methodist movement gradually separated from the Anglican Church, and the Methodist Church emerged. After World War I, the Methodist church began work in Czechoslovakia with evangelization and providing social aid that was supported by the American Methodist Church. The Evangelical Methodist Church in Slovakia partners with the Czechs and belongs to the Central Conference in Central and South Europe. After 1993, the two regional councils were established, one in each country. Social concerns continue to dominate this ministry.

The beginnings of the Brethren Church/Presbyterian Church date back to 1860–1880 when the Free Evangelical Czech Church and Free Reformed Church merged to become the Brethren Unity. The Presbyterian system of administration was implemented, and the church expanded to Slovakia. When the country split, two independent churches came into being. As of 1999, the church in Slovakia had nine congregations, thirty preaching stations, and 2,125 members.

Although these churches represent the larger congregational memberships, many minority denominations are active and growing in the country.

The World Council of Churches plays a key role in promoting Christian unity in Slovakia and many denominations play an active part. During a time of continued development and transformation, representatives meet regularly as an Ecumenical Council to assist and consider their roles in the process.

Slovakia's Wooden Churches

Drawing by Sarah Krueger

Built in 1875, the Tserkva of the Mother of God Church is in Hraničné, Slovakia.

In 1681, Austro-Hungarian Emperor, Franz Josef, being of the Roman Catholic faith, made into law that only Roman Catholics could use stone or metal in constructing churches. Any Protestant or Ruthenian/Rusyn Greek Catholic churches had to be made of wood. The use of metal nails was prohibited and thus the Emperor believed he had control over the growing number of Protestant and Ruthenian/Rusyn Greek Catholic churches being built. Further, they had to be completely finished within one year's time, and were not allowed to be built in the center of a village or town.

This set the imaginative forces of gifted designers and carpenters into action. Many of the beautiful wooden churches, held together with wooden pegs and other techniques, still stand. These churches, most prevalent in the northeastern corner of Slovakia, are intricate in design and style and remarkably well preserved.

A Slovak Easter

The Easter celebration, or *Vel'káNoc* (The Great Night), brings many more customs to the fore in Slovakia. One tradition that still prevails throughout the land is the presence of the large family Easter basket. Filled with a variety of palatable items, one may find *paska* or *babka* (a special bread), butter, smoked sausage, cooked ham, beet horseradish, smoked slab bacon, hard-boiled eggs, and salt. In eastern Slovakia, a regional delicacy called *syrek* (the little cheese) is included in the basket. Other items may include poppy seed or nut rolls, wine, and special decorated eggs. The basket is lined with a lovely piece of needlework or embroidered cloth and covered with another fancy needlework design to enhance the beauty of the basket.

In the Western and Central parts of Slovakia, *kraslice* eggs are added. These eggs are colored and decorated with scratched designs. *Pisanky* eggs may also be included in Eastern Slovakia and are decorated by several different methods. Eggs hold great significance in the lore of Slovakia, and are traditionally decorated and exchanged around the time of the spring equinox. At one time, they were regarded as powerful symbols and charms guarding against evil and it was believed that they brought good fortune to the recipients.

Blessed candles are included in the baskets in some regions. On the Saturday before Easter Sunday, after the basket is prepared, it is taken in a ceremonial procession through the village to a central place and blessed by the local priest. Then it could be consumed by the family on Easter Sunday morning, thus breaking the Lenten fast. During the procession, the streets are lined with young people, boys on one side and girls on the other.

Burning candles, to celebrate the coming Resurrection of Christ, illuminate the windows in homes along the way. The Blessed Sacrament is carried by the priest leading the procession, and church bells are rung when the procession reaches the village church.

Traditionally, on Easter Sunday afternoon and Monday, the boys "switch" the girls and throw water on them. This is still done today in many parts of Slovakia, but the practice has taken on variations. It is said the girls run away so as not to get wet, but they do not run too fast or too far. The more times a girl has to change clothes, the more popular she is. The "switching" whip was made of braided willow branches and decorated with colorful ribbons. In some places, only the water dousing is done and in some only the "switching." In Bratislava, tradition calls for the boys to do the "switching" on Easter Sunday; in other places, it is done on Easter Monday, and the girls do the "switching." Whichever way it is done, it is done in harmless fun, and the boys go from house to house being fed and entertained in the process. Easter dinner in the Slovak home usually includes lamb or ham as the main course. In some homes, pork roast with dumplings and sauerkraut is the main meal. This depends on locality and personal family traditions. In our home, we most usually had roast goose or pork roast, both served with sauerkraut and dumplings. One thing is certain: there is never a shortage of homemade bakery to finish off the meal. After celebrating Easter Sunday with church observations and the large Easter dinner, the celebration continues through Easter Monday with friends and relatives. Exchanging colored, decorated eggs, gifts, enjoying music, and getting caught up on family news until late in the evening, the special Easter holiday is then brought to a close.

An antique postcard showing switching, an Easter custom.

Spring Comes to Slovakia

© 1998 horned goddess, by Sidonka Wadina

In Slovakia, in spring, a ritual was performed by Slovak women called the bringing of "new summer." A flowering branch or small tree was adorned with ribbons and eggs; a goddess figure was placed at the top. The figure was made of plaited straw, arms in the orant position, invoking, begging for sun and rain; bringing this decorated tree into the village signaled the return of summer and the season of fertility.

The goddess figure pictured above sprouts a smaller figure, symbol of new life, within her body, stressing the fertility of the goddess. On her upraised arms rest birds, which in ancient culture symbolized the divine soul; many of the earliest examples of spring goddesses are coupled with birds. The orant position, upraised arms, is one of the most characteristic poses. The birds hold in their beaks golden rings, a symbol of the sun, which they carry to earth. The image of the goddess is further enhanced when coupled with the tree of life motif. "Branches" from the base of the goddess join her hands and she appears tree-like.

In Slovakia, women wore horns made of wood or metal under their headdresses or braided their hair and shaped it to give the appearance of horns, called *rohe*. In some villages, women rolled their kerchiefs to look like horns; some bridal headdresses had large, rigid, horn-like projections. Horns were a symbol of women's power; the power of fertility and the continuity of life.

Finally, two birds perch on the branch-like arms of the tree of life, bringing the nourishment of the sun to the horned goddess for the benefit of the new life that sprouts within her body.

—Sidonka Wadina

About the Author: Toni Brendel

Toni Brendel has spent a lifetime exploring her roots and this book reflects a Slovak family history symbolic of many of the immigrants who came from Eastern Europe. As a founding member and former President of the Phillips Wisconsin Czechoslovakian Community Festival, Toni has served as a chair or co-chair of the festival for 23 of its 25 years.

She co-produced the first two volumes of the *Phillips Czechoslovakian Community History* and is currently working on the 25th anniversary volume. Toni authored the brochure, *Lidice Shall Live in Phillips, Wisconsin*, which is widely circulated. She is the writer of numerous articles in the *Wisconsin Slovak* magazine.

Toni Brendel has served as the State Director of the Miss Czech-Slovak Wisconsin Queen Pageant held annually in Phillips for 10 years and is a member of the board of directors for the Miss Czech-Slovak US Queen Pageant held in Wilber, Nebraska, each August. She has served as a judge for the Minnesota Miss Czech-Slovak State Pageant on several occasions. She holds memberships in the Wisconsin Slovak Historical Society, Price County Historical Society, Czechoslovak Genealogical Society International, Western Fraternal Life Association (Phillips Lodge #236,) Slovak Heritage and Folklore Society International, SVU (Czechoslovak Society of Arts and Sciences), and the National Czech & Slovak Museum & Library.

Toni's contributions to her community go far beyond her Slovak roots. In 2002, she was named *Phillips Citizen of the Year* and was the first woman to serve on the Board of Directors of the Phillips Area Chamber of Commerce. She is currently the proprietress of the Phillips High School Alumni Tourist House.

As a mother of five, grandmother of six, she continues to be active in church, school, and civic affairs.

—Jacque Gharib, editor

Listing of Recipes

Ashley Brown, Slovak girl, former Miss Czech-Slovak Wisconsin State Princess, is shown in her Trenčín kroj. She started a program for younger girls interested in the Miss Czech-Slovak Wisconsin State Queen Pageant. Ashley volunteered to assist the annual dinner of the International Studies Program at UW-Stevens Point. A college student, she has studied abroad in several nations.

Below: *The Karpato-Rusyn Ensemble of Cleveland performed at St. Michael's Byzantine Catholic Church in Akron, Ohio in 2007. The director is Laurel A Tombazzi.*

Joe Wadowick photograph

Books by Mail (Prices are subject to change.)

$18.95 *Slovak American Touches (this book)*

$12.95 *Fairy Tales of Eastern Europe*

$12.95 *Key of Gold, 23 Czech Fairy Tales*

$12.95 *Prague Saints and Heroes of the Charles Bridge*

$12.95 *Czech and Slovak Touches*

Postage and handling

$6.95	Under $25.00
$9.95	$25.01–$50.00
$12.95	$50.01–$75.00
$15.95	$75.00 and over

Books sent to more than one address, add shipping and handling separately for each address. Wholesale orders for non-profit groups and others are billed for shipping.

Wisconsin or Iowa residents add sales tax.

Stocking Stuffers *(Small spiral bound recipe books. Use this schedule for shipping costs).* (1 postpaid $12.00; 2 for $20; 3 for $28; 4 for $35; 6 for $50; 12 for $90.00)

Slavic Specialties, Czech & Slovak Kolaches & Sweet Treats, Cherished Czech Recipes, Quality Dumpling Recipes, Quality Czech Mushroom Recipes

Please send $2.50 for a complete catalog of all titles. Retailers and cultural fund raisers please call or send for wholesale discounts.

Please pay by personal check or by credit card: Visa, Master Charge, Discover, American Express

Toni Brendel
1-715-339-3629
FAX 1-715-339-3629
EMAIL: brendel@pctcnet.net
336 North Lake Avenue
Phillips, Wisconsin 54555
(Please ask about autographed copies of *Slovak Amerian Touches* by Toni)

Penfield Books
EMAIL Penfield@penfieldbooks.com
1-800-728-9998 FAX 319-351-6846
215 Brown Street
Iowa City, Iowa 52245

Dr. Martin Meša photograph

Slovak bridal group in kroje *from Hont*

The designer of the present-day Slovak State Coat of Arms is painter Ladislav Čisárik, Jr. Its official interpretation: the Lorraine cross symbolizes St.Benedict, St.Cyril, and St. Methodius. The three hills are interpreted as the Tatra, Matra, and Fatra mountains.

This present form was enacted on March 1, 1990 in the constitutional law of Slovak National Council and made into law February 18, 1993.

Poland

Czech Republic

Tatra Mtns.

Carpathian Mtns.

Prešov •

Košice •

Slovak Republic

Ukraine

Austria

• Bratislava

Danube River

Hungary